PAKISTAN 2016 HUMAN RIGHTS REPORT

EXECUTIVE SUMMARY

Pakistan is a federal republic. In May 2013 the Pakistan Muslim League-Nawaz (PML-N) party won a majority of seats in parliamentary elections, and Nawaz Sharif became prime minister for the third time. While judged to be mostly free and fair, some independent observers and political parties raised concerns about election irregularities. Asif Ali Zardari completed his five-year term as president in September 2013 with Mamnoon Hussain (PML-N) succeeding him. Orderly transitions in the military (chief of army staff) and the judiciary (Supreme Court chief justice) solidified the democratic transition.

Civilian authorities generally maintained effective control over the security forces.

The most serious human rights problems were extrajudicial and targeted killings; disappearances; torture; lack of rule of law (including lack of due process, poor implementation and enforcement of laws, and frequent mob violence and vigilante justice); gender inequality; violence against gender and sexual minorities; and sectarian violence.

Other human rights problems included poor prison conditions, arbitrary detention, lengthy pretrial detention, a weak criminal justice system, lack of judicial independence in the lower courts, and governmental infringement on citizens' privacy rights. Harassment of journalists continued, with high-profile attacks against journalists and media organizations. There were government restrictions on freedom of assembly and limits on freedom of movement. Government practices and certain laws limited freedom of religion, particularly for religious minorities. Discrimination against religious minorities, and sectarian violence continued. Corruption within the government and police, as well as rape, domestic violence, sexual harassment, honor crimes, other harmful traditional practices, and discrimination against women and girls remained serious societal problems. Gender inequality continued. Child abuse and commercial sexual exploitation of children persisted. Child labor remained pervasive. Widespread human trafficking, including forced and bonded labor, continued. Societal discrimination against national, ethnic, and racial minorities persisted, as did discrimination based on caste, sexual orientation, gender identity, and HIV status. Respect for worker rights was minimal.

Lack of government accountability remained a problem, and abuses often went unpunished, fostering a culture of impunity among the perpetrators whether official or unofficial. Authorities seldom punished government officials for human rights violations.

Continuing terrorist violence and human rights abuses by nonstate actors contributed significantly to human rights challenges in the country. The military continued significant campaigns against militant and terrorist groups. Nevertheless, violence, abuse, and social and religious intolerance by militant organizations and other nonstate actors located in the country and from neighboring countries contributed to a culture of lawlessness in some parts of the country, particularly in the provinces of Balochistan, Sindh, Khyber Pakhtunkhwa (KP), and the Federally Administered Tribal Areas (FATA). According to the South Asia Terrorism Portal (SATP), during the year there were 1,720 fatalities from terrorism, compared with 3,682 fatalities in 2015. Terror-related fatalities have been declining in the country since 2009, when fatalities totaled 11,704.

Section 1. Respect for the Integrity of the Person, Including Freedom from:

a. Arbitrary Deprivation of Life and other Unlawful or Politically Motivated Killings

There were numerous reports that authorities committed arbitrary or unlawful killings. Security forces reportedly committed extrajudicial killings in connection with conflicts in Punjab, Balochistan, FATA, Sindh, and KP (see section 1.g.).

Physical abuse while in official custody allegedly caused the death of some criminal suspects. Lengthy trial delays and failure to discipline and prosecute those responsible for killings contributed to a culture of impunity.

On May 1-2, Muttahida Quami Movement (MQM) officials alleged that the Sindh Rangers illegally detained and tortured an MQM worker who died in custody in Karachi. Chief of Army Staff Raheel Sharif ordered an inquiry into the incident. The director general of the Sindh Rangers suspended five officers for their alleged involvement in the MQM worker's death.

There were continued allegations of politically motivated killings of Baloch nationalists in Balochistan and Sindh. In his testimony before the Senate of Pakistan Standing Committee on Human Rights, Balochistan's Frontier Corps Deputy Inspector General for Investigations and Crime declared that 1,040 persons had been killed in Balochistan in 2015-16. He claimed there was "no evidence of security agency involvement" in the killings.

The SATP reported that journalists, teachers, students, and human rights defenders also were targeted by state and nonstate actors in Balochistan. According to the SATP, as of November 20, at least 244 civilians were killed in Balochistan, compared with 247 during 2015.

On August 8, a coordinated attack in Quetta killed at least 73 individuals, 55 of them lawyers. Both Da'esh and the Pakistani Taliban (TTP) splinter group Jamaat-ul-Ahrar claimed responsibility for the attack.

There were reports of politically motivated killings by political factions or unknown assailants in Sindh. On May 8, gunmen killed a well-known activist and journalist, Khurram Zaki, in Karachi. The Tehreek-e-Taliban (TTP) Hakeemullah Mehsud Group claimed credit for the attack and said it was retribution for the media campaign he ran against the Islamabad-based Red Mosque cleric Maulana Abdul Aziz. On June 22, gunmen killed Amjad Sabri, a well-known Sufi qawali (Sufi devotional music) singer in a targeted attack in Karachi. According to media reports, the TTP Hakeemullah Mehsud Group claimed responsibility for the killing, calling the Sufi music "blasphemous." Police and security agencies arrested several MQM members, who reportedly confessed to involvement in the Sabri murder.

The provincial government and political parties in Sindh, Balochistan, KP, and Punjab remained targets of attack by militant and other nonstate actors.

On July 24 unidentified militants killed a senior cleric from the Jamiat Ulema Islam-Fazlur (JUI-F), a coalition partner of the ruling PML-N, and his son in Balochistan's Kech District. In March the bodies of five government employees who had been abducted in Kech district were found. All the victims were employees of the Urban Planning and Development Department. On January 22, Balochistan Home Minister Mir Sarfaraz Ahmed Bugti (PML-N) narrowly escaped an assassination attempt when his convoy hit a roadside bomb in Dera Bugti, Balochistan. Bugti survived another attempt on his life near Sui, Balochistan, on February 29.

In October hundreds of sleeping police recruits were attacked at a police academy in Quetta, Balochistan. Suicide bombers killed 61 cadets and injured 117. Da'esh claimed responsibility, but security officials told media that Lashkar-e-Jhangvi was behind the attack.

District-level and provincial politicians from Awami National Party, Pakistan People's Party, Pakistan Tehreek-e-Insaaf (PTI), and JUI-F were shot and killed in targeted attacks throughout KP and FATA. On April 25, PTI provincial assembly member Sardar Soran Singh (from the minority Sikh community) was killed by gunmen in KP's Buner District. Police alleged the killing was politically motivated, ordered by a rival Sikh politician who stood to inherit Singh's reserved seat in the Provincial Assembly.

Militants and terrorist groups killed hundreds and injured thousands with bombs, suicide attacks, and other violence (see section 1.g.).

The government ended its moratorium on capital punishment in 2014, following the attack on the Army Public School in Peshawar. Human rights organizations reported concerns with observance of due process and the execution of individuals under age 18 when they allegedly committed the crime.

b. Disappearance

There were kidnappings and forced disappearances of persons from various backgrounds in nearly all areas of the country. Some police and security forces reportedly held prisoners incommunicado and refused to disclose their location. Human rights organizations reported many Sindhi and Baloch nationalists as among the missing; for example, the International Voice for Baloch Missing Persons (a separate organization from the VBMP) in August claimed that forced disappearance victims were being killed by security forces in contrived police encounters.

Karachi-based political party MQM alleged that the paramilitary Sindh Rangers kidnapped, tortured, and killed some of its members in security operations in Karachi. They claimed authorities killed 61 MQM members extrajudicially in the operations. In May the MQM submitted to the Supreme Court a list of 171 political workers who it said had been missing since January. The party said Sindh Rangers were responsible for abducting party workers. The Human Rights Commission of Pakistan (HRCP) called for a probe into extrajudicial killings and disappearances of MQM workers. Nationalist parties in Sindh also alleged that law enforcement agencies kidnapped and killed Sindhi political activists. Jeay Sindh Muttahida Mahaz (JSMM), a banned Sindhi nationalist party, claimed that during 2016, 11 of their party members had been abducted by security agencies across Sindh. In April, a senior nationalist leader and founder of Jiye Sindh Tehreek, Shafi Karnani, was shot and killed in Thatta, Sindh by unknown assailants.

The Commission of Inquiry on Enforced Disappearances headed by Supreme Court Justice Javed Iqbal and retired law enforcement official Muhammad Sharif Virt received 3,522 missing persons cases between 2011 and July 31. The commission claimed to have closed out 2,105 of those cases and to have traced 1,614 of the missing persons, while 1,417 of the cases remained open.

According to press reporting and human rights groups, a Karachi-based Baloch activist was abducted by alleged security officials when he stopped at a highway toll plaza on July 26; he was released in December. The National Commission on Human Rights (NCHR) opened an investigation, but there were no additional details regarding his abduction as of the end of the year.

In January the Peshawar High Court dismissed the case of Indian citizen Hamid Nehal Ansari, pending since 2012, when the Ministry of Defense confirmed to the Commission of Inquiry on Enforced Disappearances that Ansari was in the army's custody pending trial before a military court. According to media reports, he was convicted of espionage and sentenced to three years' imprisonment in February. According to Ansari's mother, the Mumbai native was job seeking in Afghanistan when he crossed into Kohat, KP, to meet a woman he had met online before being arrested at his hotel.

The VBMP claimed the total number of persons who had disappeared since 2000 in Balochistan could be greater than 20,000. The International Voice for Baloch Missing Persons maintained an online database of missing persons in Balochistan, and it listed a total of 739 individuals missing since 1969, including 100 individuals who allegedly were abducted during the year.

There were reports of disappearances in connection with continuing conflicts between militant groups and government forces in Punjab and FATA.

c. Torture and Other Cruel, Inhuman, or Degrading Treatment or Punishment

Although the constitution prohibits torture and other cruel, inhuman, or degrading treatment, the criminal code has no specific section against torture. It prohibits causing "hurt" but does not mention punishing perpetrators of torture. There are no legislative provisions specifically prohibiting torture. There were reports that security forces, including the intelligence services, tortured and abused individuals in custody.

According to the Asian Human Rights Commission, the absence of proper complaint centers and the absence of a particular section in the criminal code that defines and prohibits torture contributed to such practices. The commission maintained that the government undertook no serious effort to make torture a crime and that perpetrators, mostly police or members of the armed forces, operated with impunity.

There were reports some police personnel employed cruel and degrading treatment and punishment. The HRCP reported that police committed acts they described as "police excesses" in more than 124 cases as of November, compared with more than 178 cases in 2015. Multiple sources reported that torture occasionally resulted in death or serious injury and was often underreported. Acts described by Society for Human Rights and Prisoners' Aid (SHARP) and other human rights organizations included beating with batons and whips, burning with cigarettes, whipping the soles of feet, prolonged isolation, electric shock, denying food or sleep, hanging upside down, and forced spreading the legs with bar fetters.

In March the newspaper *Dawn* reported that Manzoor Shah died three days after he was transferred to Karachi Central Prison after allegedly being tortured by police while in custody. An MQM senator said Shah was arrested by paramilitary forces and then handed over to prison authorities after the end of his remand period. According to the postmortem, Shah died from a head injury caused by a hard and blunt object.

The practice of collective punishment continued in FATA and the Provincially Administered Tribal Areas (PATA), as provided for in the 114-year-old "Frontier Crimes Regulation" (FCR), which governs FATA. In 2011 the government amended the FCR to exempt women, all individuals over age 65, and children below age 16 from collective punishment. Authorities apply collective punishment incrementally, starting with the first immediate male family members, followed by the subtribe, and continuing outward. Although this graduated approach reduces its scope, the FCR assigns collective punishment without regard to individual rights. Human rights nongovernmental organizations (NGOs) expressed concern about the concept of collective responsibility, as authorities used collective responsibility to detain members of fugitives' tribes, demolish their homes, confiscate or destroy their property, or lay siege to fugitive villages pending surrender or punishment by fugitives' own tribes in accordance with local tradition. In November media and local government officials reported security forces demolished a market in Wana, South Waziristan, near the Afghan border in an attribution of "collective responsibility" following the death of a military officer by an improvised explosive device during a raid on the market conducted against militants.

Military Operations in the FATA continued throughout the year, targeting militant groups, primarily in Waziristan. Restrictions on access to these conflict zones imposed by the government limited the information available to international observers, including the United Nations, civil society, and nongovernmental actors about possible abuses in these areas.

Pakistan has a total of 7,156 police, military experts, and soldiers performing peacekeeping duties around the world. The United Nations reported that during the year (as of December 20) it received two allegations of sexual exploitation and abuse against Pakistani peacekeepers for one alleged incident occurring during the year and for one of which the date was unknown. One allegation involved military personnel deployed to the UN Operation in Cote d'Ivoire, was being investigated by the government and allegedly involved minors. There was no result by the end of the year. The other allegation, involving military personnel deployed to the UN Multidimensional Integrated Stabilization Mission in the Central African Republic, was investigated by the government and found to be unsubstantiated.

Prison and Detention Center Conditions

Conditions in some prisons and detention centers were harsh and life threatening. Problems such as overcrowding and inadequate medical care were widespread.

Physical Conditions: Prison conditions often were extremely poor. Overcrowding was common. SHARP estimated the nationwide prison population at 100,000 while claiming that the normal capacity of prisons was approximately 36,000.

Provincial governments were the primary managers of prisons and detention centers, after those run by the national government and the military.

Inadequate food and medical care in prisons led to chronic health problems and malnutrition among inmates unable to supplement their diets with help from family or friends. In many facilities sanitation, ventilation, lighting, and access to potable water were inadequate. Most prison facilities were antiquated and had no means to control indoor temperatures. A system existed for basic and emergency medical care, but bureaucratic procedures slowed access. Foreign prisoners often remained in prison long after completion of their sentences because they were unable to pay for deportation to their home countries.

Prison security remained a concern. Media reported that a prison break in Mardan, KP, occurred in June; however, prison officials denied there were any escapees, and no further information was available.

Prisoners who were members of religious minorities generally received poorer facilities than Muslims and often suffered violence at the hands of fellow inmates. Representatives of Christian and Ahmadiyya Muslim communities claimed their members were often subjected to abuse in prison. Civil society organizations reported prisoners accused of blasphemy violations were frequently subjected to poor prison conditions. NGOs reported that many individuals accused of blasphemy remained in solitary confinement for extended periods, sometimes for more than a year. The government asserted this treatment was for the individual's safety.

Authorities held women separately from men in some, but not all, prisons. Balochistan had no women's prison; officials claimed they housed women in separate barracks in Quetta and Lasbela district prisons.

Police often did not segregate detainees from convicted criminals. Prisoners with mental disabilities usually lacked adequate care.

Prison officials usually kept juvenile offenders in barracks separate from adults. Nevertheless, officials often mixed children with the general prison population at some point during their imprisonment. According to the Society for the Protection of the Rights of the Child (SPARC), prisoners and prison staff often subjected children to abuse, rape, and other forms of violence.

According to SPARC, authorities sometimes held juvenile prisoners mixed with the general population in prisons in all four provinces and FATA.

SPARC described conditions for juvenile prisoners as among the worst in the country. Many juveniles spent long periods behind bars because they could not afford bail. According to SPARC, rather than being rehabilitated, child prisoners often became hardened criminals after having spent long periods in the company of adult prisoners.

The Juvenile Justice System Ordinance, which outlines the treatment of juveniles in the justice system, does not apply to juveniles accused of terrorism or narcotics offenses. SPARC reported that in the past, officials arrested children as young as age 12 on charges of terrorism under the Antiterrorism Act. Children convicted under the act could be sentenced to death. There were numerous cases of individuals on death row having been convicted of crimes allegedly committed, and/or tried for, while under the age of 18. Lack of documentation continued to be a challenge for verifying questions of legal age. Civil society sources reported that while they had no official reports of current juvenile inmates on death row, they could not rule out the possibility. Different courts made different decisions as to what was "adequate" proof of age.

Administration: According to SHARP, there was adequate manual recordkeeping on prisoners, but there was a need for computerized records. In July the reported that a digitized Prison Management Information System was operational in 20 prisons in Punjab.

There was an ombudsman for detainees, with a central office in Islamabad and offices in each province. Inspectors general of prisons irregularly visited prisons and detention facilities to monitor conditions and handle complaints.

By law prison authorities must permit prisoners and detainees to submit complaints to judicial authorities without censorship and to request investigation of credible allegations of inhuman conditions. According to SHARP, however, prisoners often refrained from submitting complaints to avoid retaliation from jail authorities.

The constitution mandates that religious minority prisoners must be accorded places to worship inside jails. It was unclear to what extent authorities implemented this provision.

Independent Monitoring: International organizations responsible for monitoring prisons reported difficulty accessing detention sites, in particular those holding security-related detainees. Authorities did not allow international organizations access to detention centers most affected by violence in KP, FATA, and Balochistan. Provincial governments in Sindh, Gilgit-Baltistan, and Azad Jammu Kashmir (AJK) permitted some international organizations to monitor civil prisons, but leaders of monitoring organizations noted that their operations were becoming more restricted each year.

Authorities at the local, provincial, and national levels permitted some human rights groups and journalists to monitor prison conditions of juveniles and female inmates.

d. Arbitrary Arrest or Detention

The law prohibits arbitrary arrest and detention, but authorities did not always comply. Corruption and impunity compounded this problem.

On April 23, law enforcement officials arrested Sindh nationalist party Jeay Sindh Qaumi Muhaz (JSQM) activist Kehar Ansari, which JSQM claimed was arbitrary and designed to sabotage their organization. On May 2, JSQM members organized a protest calling for Ansari's release. Law enforcement agencies broke up the protest, injuring six and killing one protester, according to press reports. Ansari was released on May 4.

Role of the Police and Security Apparatus

Police have primary domestic security responsibility for most of the country. Local police are under the jurisdiction of provincial governments. The Rangers are a paramilitary organization under the authority of the Ministry of Interior, with branches in Sindh and Punjab. The Frontier Corps is the Rangers' counterpart in Balochistan and the tribal areas; it reports to the Ministry of Interior in peacetime and military in times of conflict. The military is responsible for external security but continues to play a role in domestic security.

The FCR provides the framework for law and order in FATA, implemented through appointed political agents who report to the governor of KP. The court system and judiciary do not have jurisdiction in FATA. Under the FCR the trial by jirga (gathering of tribal leaders) does not allow residents legal representation. If the accused is an adult male, he normally appears before the jirga in person to defend his case. Parents normally represent their minor children, and men normally represent their female relatives. Observers often criticized the FCR for harsh provisions. In 2011 authorities amended some of these provisions, including modifying the collective responsibility of a tribe, restricting the arbitrary nature of the powers of political agents or district coordination officers, and granting citizens

limited rights to challenge the decisions of political agents in a codified tribunal
system.

In lieu of police, multiple law enforcement entities operated in FATA. They
included the paramilitary Frontier Corps; the Frontier Constabulary, which patrols
the area between FATA and KP and also operates in FATA; Khasadars (hereditary
tribal police); and FATA levies, which report to the political agent to help maintain
order. Tribal leaders convene lashkars (tribal militias) to deal with temporary law
and order disturbances, but they operate as private tribal militias and not as formal
law enforcement entities.

Police effectiveness varied by district, ranging from good to ineffective.

Failure to punish abuses contributed to a climate of impunity throughout the
country. According to civil society sources, police and prison officials frequently
used the threat of abuse to extort money from prisoners and their families. The
inspectors general, district police, district nazims (chief elected officials of local
governments), provincial interior or chief ministers, federal interior minister, prime
minister, or courts can order internal investigations into abuses and order
administrative sanctions. Executive branch and police officials have authority to
recommend, and the courts may order, criminal prosecution. The court system
remained the only means available to investigate abuses by security forces. The
NCHR, established in 2015, may not inquire into any complaints against
intelligence agencies and must refer such complaints to the competent authority
concerned. The NCHR may seek a report from the national government on any
complaint made against the armed forces, and after receipt of a report, it can either
end the process or forward recommendations for further action to the national
government.

During the year the government continued to use the military to support domestic
security. Paramilitary forces, including Rangers and the Frontier Constabulary
(FC), provided security to some areas of Islamabad and continued active
operations in Karachi. Following the March 27 Easter suicide bombing attack on
Lahore's Gulshan-e-Iqbal Park, which killed 75 individuals, the military launched
a limited counterterrorism offensive in southern Punjab, which resulted in the
arrest of more than 200 suspected militants, although much of the military's effort
focused on criminal gangs in the area. In May the International Crisis Group
assessed in a special report on Jihadist groups operating in southern Punjab that the
military campaign did not target certain militant groups, and instead carried out a
21-day operation against the Chotu criminal gang located in the Rajanpur district

of Punjab. Paramilitary FC forces continued active security operations in Balochistan.

In January 2015, in response to a terrorist attack on the Peshawar Army Public School, Parliament approved a constitutional amendment to allow military courts to try civilians on terrorism, militancy, sectarian violence, and other charges. The amendment included a provision under which the courts would expire in January 2017. In August 2015 the Supreme Court upheld this use of military courts while retaining its own right to review cases. NGOs, opposition leaders, and activists expressed concerns about the use of military courts for civilian suspects, citing lack of transparency and its redundancy with the civilian judicial system. On August 29, the Supreme Court upheld the death sentences for 16 civilians convicted of terrorism by the military courts.

Police often failed to protect members of religious minorities--including Christians, Ahmadiyya Muslims, Shi'a Muslims, and Hindus--from attacks. There were improvements, however, in police professionalism and instances of local authorities protecting minorities from discrimination and communal violence. During the year at least 20 members from these communities were killed; in April allegations that a Christian man had blasphemous videos on his cell phone led to a mob forming and attempting to burn houses in the Christian community of Chak 44 in northern Punjab. Ten Christian families fled. A deployment of an additional 70 police officers and the coordinated messaging of a local "peace committee" of Christians and Muslims helped to disperse the mob and diffuse tensions. In May, Christians near Gujrat used an emergency police hotline when a mob formed after a local cleric tried to file blasphemy charges against a young Christian woman. Police and community members worked to diffuse the situation, and ultimately the cleric withdrew the complaint. As in previous years, the Punjab provincial government conducted regular training in technical skills and protection of human rights for police at all levels.

On December 12, a mob of approximately 1,000 persons attacked an Ahmadi mosque in Chakwal, Punjab, throwing stones and firing rounds at the building. Police eventually dispersed the crowds. There were reports that one Ahmadi died of a heart attack, and one member was killed during the attack; police arrested multiple Ahmadies on murder charges as a result. The Ahmadis' local leadership had written to the district and provincial government one week earlier requesting security for the mosque due to local religious clerics' incitements of violence against the site.

Arrest Procedures and Treatment of Detainees

A First Information Report (FIR) is the legal basis for any arrest, initiated when police receive information about the commission of a "cognizable" offense. A third party usually initiates an FIR, but police can file FIRs on their own initiative. A FIR allows police to detain a suspect for 24 hours, after which a magistrate may order detention for an additional 14 days if police show detention is necessary to obtain evidence material to the investigation. Some authorities did not observe these limits on detention. Authorities reportedly filed FIRs without supporting evidence in order to harass or intimidate detainees, or did not file them when adequate evidence was provided unless the complainant paid a bribe. There were reports of persons arrested without judicial authorization.

NGOs reported that individuals frequently paid bribes to visit prisoners. The Ministry of Interior frequently did not provide notification of the arrest of foreigners to their respective embassies or consulates. In 2015 the ministry introduced a new requirement that foreign missions request access to their arrested citizens 20 days in advance.

There was a functioning bail system. Human rights groups, noted, however, that some judges set bail based on the particular circumstances of a case instead of following established procedures. Judges sometimes denied bail at the request of police or the community and victims, or upon payment of bribes. NGOs reported that authorities sometimes denied bail in blasphemy cases on the grounds that defendants, who faced the death penalty, were likely to flee or were at risk from public vigilantism. Bail is not available in antiterrorism courts or in the military courts established under the January 2015 amendment to the constitution.

The government provided state-funded legal counsel to prisoners facing the death penalty, but it did not regularly provide legal representation in other cases. NGOs provided legal aid in some cases. The constitution recognizes the right of habeas corpus and allows the high courts to demand a person accused of a crime be present in court. The law allows citizens to submit habeas corpus petitions to the courts. In many cases involving forced disappearances, authorities failed to present detainees according to judges' orders.

<u>Arbitrary Arrest</u>: There were reports police arbitrarily detained individuals to extort bribes for their release or detained relatives of wanted individuals to compel suspects to surrender.

<u>Pretrial Detention</u>: Police sometimes held persons in investigative detention without seeking a magistrate's approval and often held detainees without charge until a court challenged the detention. Magistrates generally approved investigative detention at the request of police without requiring justification. When police did not develop sufficient evidence to try a suspect within the 14-day period, police generally requested that magistrates issue new FIRs, thereby further extending the suspect's detention.

By law detainees must be brought to trial within 30 days of arrest. There were exceptions; a district coordination officer has authority to recommend preventive detention on the grounds of "maintenance of public order" for up to 90 days and may--with approval of the Home Department--extend it for an additional 90 days.

In some cases trials did not start until six months after the FIR, and at times individuals remained in pretrial detention for periods longer than the maximum sentence for the crime with which they were charged. SHARP estimated that more than 70 percent of the prison population was awaiting trial. Authorities seldom informed detainees promptly of charges against them.

Special rules apply to cases brought to court by the National Accountability Bureau (NAB), which investigates and prosecutes corruption cases. The NAB may detain suspects for 15 days without charge (renewable with judicial concurrence) and deny access to counsel prior to charging. Offenses under the NAB are not bailable, and only the NAB chairman has the power to decide whether to release detainees.

Under the FCR in FATA, the political agent has legal authority to detain preventively individuals on a variety of grounds and may require bonds to prevent undesired activities. Indefinite detention is not allowed, and detained persons may appeal to the FCR tribunal. Prisoners have the right to compensation for wrongful punishment. Cases must be decided within a specified period, and authorities may release arrested persons on bail. Regulations require prisoners to be brought before FCR authorities within 24 hours of detention, which curtails the ability of political agents to arbitrarily arrest and hold persons for up to three years. The accused have the right of appeal via a two-tiered system, which starts with an appellate authority comprising an FCR commissioner and an additional judicial commissioner.

In FATA, PATA, and KP, security forces may restrict the activities of terrorism suspects, seize their assets for up to 48 hours, and detain them for as long as one year without charges. Human rights and international organizations reported that authorities held an unknown number of individuals allegedly affiliated with terrorist organizations indefinitely in preventive detention, where they were often tortured and abused. In many cases authorities held prisoners incommunicado, denying them prompt access to a lawyer of their choice. Family members often were not allowed prompt access to detainees.

A 2011 Regulation provides the military a legal framework to operate in conflict areas. It regulates the armed forces and provides them with legal authority to handle detainees under civilian supervision when called upon by the government. Retroactive to 2008, the regulation empowers the KP governor to direct armed forces to intern suspected terrorists in FATA and PATA. Critics stated the regulation violates the constitution because of its broad provisions expanding military authority and circumventing legal due process. Detainee transfers to internment centers continued on a regular basis.

Detainee's Ability to Challenge Lawfulness of Detention before a Court: There were reports of persons arrested or detained who were not allowed to challenge in court the legal basis or nature of their detention, obtain relief, or receive compensation.

e. Denial of Fair Public Trial

The law provides for an independent judiciary, but the judiciary often was subjected to external influences, such as fear of reprisal from extremist elements in terrorism or blasphemy cases and public politicization of high-profile cases. The media and the public generally considered the high courts and the Supreme Court credible.

Extensive case backlogs in the lower and superior courts, together with other problems, undermined the right to effective remedy and to a fair and public hearing. Delays in justice in civil and criminal cases were due to antiquated procedural rules, unfilled judgeships, poor case management, and weak legal education.

The jurisdiction of the Supreme Court and the high courts does not extend to several areas that operated under separate judicial systems. For example, AJK has its own elected president, prime minister, legislature, and court system. Gilgit-Baltistan also has a separate judicial system.

Many lower courts remained corrupt, inefficient, and subject to pressure from wealthy persons and influential religious and/or political figures.

There were instances in which unknown persons threatened and/or killed witnesses, prosecutors, or investigating police officers in high-level cases. On June 21, the Sindh High Court chief justice's son, Owais Ali Shah, was abducted outside a grocery store in Karachi. Security forces rescued Shah on July 19 near the Tank district of KP.

Informal justice systems lacking institutionalized legal protections continued, especially in rural areas, and often resulted in human rights abuses. Landlords and other community leaders in Sindh and Punjab, and tribal leaders in Pashtun and Baloch areas, at times held local council meetings ("panchayats" or "jirgas"), external to the established legal system. Such councils settled feuds and imposed tribal penalties, including fines, imprisonment, and sometimes the death penalty. These councils often sentenced women to violent punishment or death for so-called honor-related crimes. In Pashtun areas, primarily in FATA, such councils were held under FCR guidelines. Assistant political agents, supported by tribal elders of their choosing, are legally responsible for justice in FATA and conduct hearings according to their interpretation of Islamic law and tribal custom.

Trial Procedures

The civil, criminal, and family court systems provide for a fair trial and due process, presumption of innocence, cross-examination, and appeal. There are no trials by jury. Although defendants have the right to be present and consult with an attorney, courts must appoint attorneys for indigents only in capital cases. Defendants generally bear the cost of legal representation in lower courts, but a lawyer may be provided at public expense in appellate courts. Defendants may confront or question prosecution witnesses and present their own witnesses and evidence. Defendants and attorneys have legal access to government-held evidence. Due to the limited number of judges, a heavy backlog of cases, lengthy court procedures, frequent adjournment, and political pressure, cases routinely lasted for years, and defendants made frequent court appearances.

SPARC reported that adjudication of cases involving juveniles was slow due to a lack of special juvenile courts or judges. It concluded that a fair and just juvenile justice system did not exist.

There were instances of lack of transparency in court cases, particularly if the case dealt with high-profile or sensitive issues. NGOs reported that the government often located trials in jails because of security concerns, which extended to the accused, lawyers, judges, prosecutors, and witnesses. NGOs expressed concerns about the security of the jail trials and lack of privacy for the accused to consult with a lawyer.

The Antiterrorism Act allows the government to use special, streamlined Antiterrorism Act Courts (ATCs) to try persons charged with violent crimes, terrorist activities, acts, or speech designed to foment religious hatred, and crimes against the state. In other courts suspects must be brought to court within seven working days of their arrest, but the ATCs are free to extend the period. Human rights activists criticized the expedited parallel system, charging that it was more vulnerable to political manipulation. In 2014, after a judge's ruling that the Antiterrorism Act had been incorrectly applied, authorities returned 15 percent of cases initially brought to ATCs to regular courts, according to Punjab's prosecutor general. NGOs reported that if a case needed to be expedited due to the egregious nature of the crime or political pressure, it was often sent to an ATC rather than through the regular court system. Others commented that, despite being comparatively faster than the regular court system, the ATCs often failed to meet speedy trial standards and had significant case backlogs.

The government continued to utilize military courts to try civilians on terrorism and related charges. Trials in military courts are not public (see section 1.d.).

The Federal Shariat Court typically reviewed cases prosecuted under the Hudood Ordinance--a law enacted in 1979 by military leader Muhammad Zia-ul-Haq to implement a strict interpretation of Islamic law by punishing extramarital sex, false accusations of extramarital sex, theft, and drinking alcohol. Should a provincial high court decide to hear an appeal in a Hudood case, the Shariat courts lack authority to review the provincial high court's decision. The Supreme Court may bypass the Shariat Appellate Bench and assume jurisdiction in such appellate cases. The Federal Shariat Court may overturn legislation judged inconsistent with Islamic tenets, but such decisions may be appealed to the Shariat Appellate Bench of the Supreme Court and ultimately may be heard by the full bench of the Supreme Court.

Courts routinely failed to protect the rights of religious minorities. Courts discriminatorily used laws prohibiting blasphemy against Shi'a, Christians, Ahmadis, and members of other religious minority groups. Lower courts often did not require adequate evidence in blasphemy cases, and some accused and convicted persons spent years in jail before higher courts eventually overturned their convictions or ordered them freed.

In 2015 the Supreme Court suspended the death sentence of Asia Bibi, a Christian woman convicted of blasphemy in 2010, pending its decision on her appeal. Bibi had been on death row since 2010 after a district court found her guilty of making derogatory remarks about the Prophet Muhammed during an argument. Her lawyers appealed to the Supreme Court in November 2014. The appeal was due to be heard on October 13 but was delayed after one member of the three-judge bench recused himself. The court did not set a date for the next hearing.

On June 20, the Lahore ATC acquitted five Christians who had been accused of blasphemy and detained since August 2015. Local police near Gujranwala had filed charges against a group of 16 individuals for allegedly publishing offensive material, and in September a Gujranwala ATC released one Muslim but denied bail to Christian defendants. Other members of the group were subsequently released on bail.

On February 29, authorities executed Mumtaz Qadri, who was convicted of killing then governor of Punjab Salmaan Taseer after Taseer had publicly called for a presidential pardon for Asia Bibi. Protests erupted after the execution, including large demonstrations in Rawalpindi that continued until March 30. Protesters, including police and lawyers, expressed support for Qadri and demanded continued enforcement of blasphemy laws.

Also see the Department of State's *International Religious Freedom Report* at www.state.gov/religiousfreedomreport/.

Political Prisoners and Detainees

Some Sindhi and Baloch nationalist groups claimed that authorities marked their members for arrest and detained them based on their political affiliation or beliefs. Under the 2009 Aghaz-e-Huqooq ("beginning of the rights") Balochistan "package," intended to address the province's political, social, and economic problems, the government announced a general amnesty for all Baloch political prisoners, leaders, and activists in exile, as well as those allegedly involved in "antistate" activities. In August 2015 the federal and Balochistan provincial governments jointly announced a new peace package called "Pur Aman Balochistan" ("peaceful Balochistan"), intended to offer cash and other incentives for "militants" who wished to rejoin mainstream society. Despite the amnesty offers, some Baloch groups claimed that illegal detention of nationalist leaders by state agencies continued. Several of the missing persons documented by the VBMP were well-known leaders of nationalist political parties and student organizations.

Civil Judicial Procedures and Remedies

Individuals may petition the courts to seek redress for various human rights violations, and courts often took such actions. Individuals may seek redress in civil courts against government officials, including on grounds of denial of human rights. Observers reported that civil courts seldom, if ever, issued official judgments in such cases, and most cases were settled out of court. Although there were no official procedures for administrative redress, informal reparations were common. Individuals and organizations could not appeal adverse decisions to regional human rights bodies, although some NGOs submitted human rights "shadow reports" to the EU and other international actors.

f. Arbitrary or Unlawful Interference with Privacy, Family, Home, or Correspondence

The law requires court-issued warrants for property searches. Police sometimes ignored this requirement and on occasion reportedly stole items during searches. Authorities seldom punished police for illegal entry. Police at times detained family members to induce a suspect to surrender. In cases pursued under the Antiterrorism Act, the government allowed security forces to search and seize property related to a case without a warrant.

Several domestic intelligence services monitored politicians, political activists, suspected terrorists, NGOs, employees of foreign entities, and the media. These services included the Inter-Services Intelligence, police Special Branch, and Military Intelligence. There were credible reports authorities routinely used wiretaps, monitored cell phone calls, intercepted electronic correspondence, and opened mail without court approval.

g. Abuses in Internal Conflict

Militant and terrorist activity continued, and there were numerous suicide and bomb attacks in all four provinces and FATA. Militants and terrorist groups, including the TTP, targeted civilians, journalists, community leaders, security forces, law enforcement agents, and schools, killing hundreds and injuring thousands with bombs, suicide attacks, and other forms of violence. Militant and terrorist groups often attacked religious minorities. A low-intensity separatist insurgency continued in Balochistan. Security forces reportedly committed extrajudicial killings in the fight against militant groups.

The military conducted multiple counterinsurgency and counterterrorism operations in FATA to eradicate militant safe havens. In 2014 the military launched Operation Zarb-e-Azb, an operation against foreign and domestic terrorists in FATA, which continued throughout the year. In the first nine months of the year, according to the SATP, the military killed more than 2,313 suspected terrorists. The government also acted throughout the country to weaken terrorist groups and prevent recruitment by militant organizations. For example, law enforcement agencies reported seizures of large caches of weapons in urban areas such as Islamabad, Lahore, and Karachi. Police arrested Karachi gang members and TTP commanders who allegedly provided logistical support to militants in the tribal areas. Police arrested would-be suicide bombers in major cities, confiscating weapons, suicide vests, and planning materials.

Poor security, intimidation by both security forces and militants, and control by government and security forces over access by nonresidents to FATA impeded the efforts of human rights organizations to provide relief to victims of military abuses and efforts of journalists to report on any such abuses.

Political, sectarian, criminal, and ethnic violence in Karachi continued, although violence declined and gang wars were less prevalent than before security operations in the city. Since 2005 natural disasters elsewhere in the country resulted in a large influx of citizens from different ethnic groups to Karachi, including ethnic Sindhi, Baloch, and Pashtun migrants, shifting the balance among political parties and the ethnic and sectarian groups they represented. Political parties and their affiliated gangs continued to vie for political and economic control, engaging in a turf war over "bhatta" (extortion) collection privileges and "ownership" over "katchi abadis" (illegal/makeshift settlements).

Killings: There were reports that government security forces caused civilian casualties and engaged in extrajudicial killings during operations against militants. Security forces killed numerous militants in Punjab and elsewhere in the country. There were numerous media reports of police and security forces killing terrorist suspects in "police encounters" nearly every week. Some observers believed security forces orchestrated at least some of these killings.

Militant and terrorist bombings in all four provinces and in FATA and PATA also killed hundreds of persons and wounded thousands. According to the SATP, until November 20, estimated terrorist and violent extremist attacks and operations to combat insurgency resulted in 1,730 deaths, of which 596 were civilians, 281 were security forces, and 853 were terrorists or insurgents.

Militants continued to target government security personnel for attack. According to the SATP, as of November 20, militants had killed 6,651 security force personnel since 2003. Military officials often quoted a much higher number, with casualties from militant attacks in the tens of thousands over the past decade.

On April 20, militants killed seven policemen guarding polio workers in two separate attacks in Orangi Town of Karachi. On January 13, a terrorist killed 15 persons, including 13 police officers and an FC soldier, in a suicide attack near a government health center in Quetta, Balochistan. The TTP claimed responsibility for the attack.

There were reports that groups prohibited by the government conducted attacks against civilians in Sindh and Balochistan. On May 30, a Sindhi separatist group, the Sindhudesh Revolutionary Army, killed a Chinese worker and his driver in a roadside bomb attack. The group opposes the development of the China-Pakistan Economic Corridor. A Baloch separatist group, the Balochistan Liberation Army, claimed responsibility for killing two persons for allegedly spying for security agencies in May and for killing another two alleged spies in June.

Sectarian violence also continued throughout the country. According to the SATP, 31 sectarian attacks from January to mid-November resulted in the deaths of 132 individuals, compared with 276 deaths in 53 incidents in 2015.

On April 6, unidentified gunmen in Dera Ismail Khan, KP, killed two lawyers and two schoolteachers, all Shia. The April 22 killing of provincial assembly member and advisor to the KP chief minister on minority affairs Sardar Soran Singh (a member of the Sikh minority) was initially claimed by the Pakistani Taliban; a subsequent police investigation indicated that a rival Sikh politician may have ordered the attack, which was political rather than sectarian in nature (see section 1.a.).

On May 5, four Shias were killed in two separate incidents in Dera Ismail Khan, prompting protests in the area. On May 7, prominent Shia civil society activist

Syed Khurram Zaki was shot in Karachi in an apparent targeted killing. On October 4, unknown gunmen boarded a bus in Quetta and shot five Hazara Shia women, killing four. On October 7, gunmen shot four Shia men in two separate incidents in Karachi, killing one.

On March 27, a suicide bomber in Lahore's Gulshan-e-Iqbal park killed 75 persons and injured more than 350, including 29 children and many victims were from Christian families who had gathered in the park for Easter Sunday. TTP splinter faction Jamaat-ul-Ahrar claimed responsibility for the bombing. Authorities subsequently arrested more than 200 suspected militants in a crackdown throughout Punjab Province.

Multiple Ahmadi community members died in what appeared to be targeted killings. Unidentified assailants stabbed an Ahmadi man to death on March 1 near Punjab's Shiekhpura district. On May 25, assailants on a motorbike shot and killed an Ahmadi man; on June 20, assailants shot an Ahmadi doctor in his clinic, with no witnesses; both killings occurred in Ahmadi community neighborhoods in Karachi. On June 4, unidentified gunmen killed an Ahmadi pharmacy owner in the city of Attock in Punjab.

Abductions: There were reports that militant groups kidnapped or took civilians hostage in FATA, KP, Punjab, Sindh, and Balochistan. In June the son of the Sindh High Court chief justice was kidnapped and subsequently rescued by a military operation in July. A military spokesman stated a splinter group of the Pakistani Taliban was responsible for the kidnapping.

In May, Ali Haider Gilani, son of former prime minister Yousuf Raza Gilani and kidnapped in 2013, was rescued during a military operation in Afghanistan. In March, Shahbaz Taseer, son of the late Punjab governor Salman Taseer, reappeared outside Quetta and claimed that he had escaped from Pakistani Taliban custody.

Physical Abuse, Punishment, and Torture: Nonstate militant groups targeted noncombatants and killed civilians in various incidents across the country.

Child Soldiers: Nonstate militant groups kidnapped boys and girls and used fraudulent promises to coerce parents into giving away children as young as age 12 to spy, fight, or die as suicide bombers. The militants sometimes offered parents money, often sexually and physically abused the children, and used psychological coercion to convince the children the acts they committed were justified. The government operated a center in Swat to rehabilitate and educate former child soldiers.

<u>Other Conflict-related Abuses</u>: Terrorist groups TTP, Lashkar-e-Jhangvi, and related factions bombed government buildings and attacked and killed female teachers and polio vaccination workers. The TTP particularly targeted girls' schools to demonstrate its opposition to girls' education; however, it also destroyed boys' schools. Military operations created hardships for the local civilian population when militants closed key access roads and tunnels and attacked communications and energy networks, disrupting commerce and the distribution of food and water.

In January terrorists killed 15 individuals in a bombing of a polio vaccination center in Quetta, Balochistan. In April terrorists killed seven police officers guarding polio health workers in an attack in Karachi. Terrorists attacked other health workers and support staff during the year, and others remained missing at year's end. The government provided armed escorts for vaccination staff to carry out polio campaigns.

Section 2. Respect for Civil Liberties, Including:

a. Freedom of Speech and Press

The law provides for freedom of speech and press, but there were constitutional restrictions. In addition, threats, harassment, violence, and killings led journalists and editors to practice self-censorship.

<u>Freedom of Speech and Expression</u>: The constitution provide for the right to free speech and the press, subject to "any reasonable restriction imposed by law in the interest of the glory of Islam" or the "integrity, security, or defense of Pakistan, friendly relations with foreign states, public order, decency or morality." The law permits citizens to criticize the government publicly or privately, but criticism of the military could result in political or commercial reprisal. Blasphemy laws restrict individual rights to free speech concerning matters of religion and religious doctrine. The government restricted some language and symbolic speech based on "hate speech" and "terrorism" provisions.

<u>Press and Media Freedoms</u>: The independent media were active and expressed a wide variety of views, and journalists often criticized the civilian portions of the government. The press addressed the persecution of minorities. By law the

government may restrict information that might be prejudicial to the national interest. Threats, harassment, and violence against journalists who reported on sensitive issues such as civil-military tensions or abuses by security forces occurred during the year.

There were 434 independent English, Urdu, and regional-language daily and weekly newspapers and magazines. To publish within AJK, media owners had to obtain permission from the Kashmir Council and the Ministry of Kashmir Affairs. The Ministry of Information and Broadcasting controlled and managed the country's primary wire service, the Associated Press of Pakistan, the official carrier of government and international news to the local media. The military had its own media and public relations office, Inter-Services Public Relations. The government-owned Pakistan Broadcasting Corporation and Pakistan Television Corporation broadcast television programs nationwide and operated radio stations throughout the country. The law does not extend to FATA or PATA, and authorities allowed independent radio stations to broadcast there with the permission of the FATA secretariat.

The Pakistan Electronic Media Regulatory Authority (PEMRA) licensed 89 private domestic and 22 foreign television channels; many of the channels were critical of the government. In July, GEO TV alleged it had been severely restricted in its broadcasting signal in Karachi for political purposes, dramatically cutting its reach in the city. GEO was restored to its previous position following the protests. There were 141 commercial FM radio stations, but their licenses prohibited news programming. Some channels evaded this restriction by discussing news in talk-show formats. International radio broadcasts, including the BBC, were normally available. There was a blockage of transmissions of Indian television news channels through late December.

PEMRA continued to prohibit media from covering the activities of any militant organization banned by the government, reportedly to bring the country into compliance with UN terrorism-related sanctions regimes. The National Action Plan also bans "the glorification of terrorism and terrorist organizations through print and electronic media." PEMRA enforced this ban throughout the year using fines. PEMRA issued editorial directives to television stations during the year and authorized its chairman to shut down any channel found in violation of the PEMRA code of conduct, primarily with regard to prohibiting telecasts of protests that might instigate sectarian violence. This included protests against the execution of Mumtaz Qadri (convicted for the murder of Punjab governor Salman Taseer over his opposition to the blasphemy law), and the Saudi government's execution of a prominent Shia cleric. PEMRA also banned television and radio outlets from broadcasting any Indian media content.

Violence and Harassment: Security forces, political parties, militants, and other groups subjected media outlets, journalists, and their families to violence and harassment. Female journalists in particular faced threats of sexual violence and harassment, including via social media. Security forces abducted journalists. Media outlets that did not practice self-censorship were often the targets of retribution. Additionally, journalists working in remote and conflict-ridden areas lacked basic digital security as well as traditional security skills, which placed additional pressure on them to self-censor or not cover a story at all.

According to the International Federation of Journalists, state and nonstate actors killed, physically attacked, harassed, intimidated and kidnapped journalists and subjected them to other forms of pressure. The Committee to Protect Journalists included the country in its annual "impunity index" because the government allowed deadly violence against members of the press to go unpunished.

In January media reported that an unidentified individual threw a grenade at offices of the private news television station ARY in Islamabad. The attack injured one person, and Da'esh claimed credit for the attack.

In March a district court in KP sentenced the killer of a journalist from the newspaper *Karak Times* murdered in 2013 to life imprisonment and a fine of $47,600. There had been only three other convictions for the murder of journalists, according to the Pakistan Press Foundation.

Censorship or Content Restriction: Small, privately owned wire services and media organizations generally reported that they engaged in self-censorship, especially in reporting news about the military forces. Journalists reported regular denial of official permission to visit conflict areas or having to be escorted either by members of the military or by militants in order to report on conditions in conflict areas. The result was pressure to produce final articles that were slanted toward the military or militant viewpoint, depending upon the escort. Other reporting tended to be relatively objective and only focused on events, rather than deeper analysis, which journalists generally regarded as risky. Observers perceived foreign journalists to have more autonomy to write about issues and to be under less scrutiny by the government. Private cable and satellite channels also reported that they censored themselves at times. Blasphemy and anti-Ahmadi laws restricted publication on certain topics. Foreign books needed to pass government censors before they could be reprinted, but there were no reports of books being banned during the year. Books and magazines could be imported freely but were subject to censorship for objectionable sexual or religious content. Obscene literature, a category the government defined broadly, was subject to seizure.

The government fined private television channels for alleged violations of the "code of ethics" and for showing banned content on-screen. Final fines depended on legal proceedings and decisions, but initial fines were between $1,000 and $10,000 per violation. The NGO Intermedia reported that state-run Pakistan Television did not operate under the purview of the law and benefitted from a monopoly on broadcast license fees. According to Freedom House, authorities used PEMRA rules to silence the broadcast media by either suspending licenses or threatening to do so. Some civil society leaders reported that military authorities frequently pressured journalists to modify the content of articles and opinion pieces critical of military actions.

Libel/Slander Laws: Ministers and members of the National Assembly used libel and slander laws in the past to counter public discussion of their actions.

National Security: Some journalists said authorities cited laws protecting national security to censor and restrict media distribution of material that criticized government policies or public officials. The 2015 Electronic Media (Programs and Advertisements) code of conduct included a clause that restricted reporting in any area that was part of a military operation in progress.

Nongovernmental Impact: Throughout the country militants and criminal elements killed, kidnapped, beat, and intimidated journalists and their families, leading many to censor their reporting. Militant and local tribal groups killed, detained, threatened, expelled, or otherwise obstructed a number of reporters who covered the conflict in FATA, KP, and Balochistan.

Internet Freedom

Since 2012 the government implemented a systematic, nationwide content-monitoring and filtering system to restrict or block "unacceptable" content, including material that is deemed un-Islamic, pornographic, or critical of the state or military forces. According to Freedom House, the government justified such restrictions as necessary for security purposes. There also were reports the government attempted to control or block some websites, including sites the government deemed extremist and proindependence Baloch sites. There was decreasing transparency and accountability surrounding content monitoring, and the government often used vague criteria without due process. In its *Freedom in the World Report* for 2016, Freedom House claimed the government blocked more than 400,000 websites due to content. The provincial government in Balochistan blocked access to a Baloch human rights blog run by journalists. The government blocked several Baloch websites, including the English-language website *The Baloch Hal* and the website of *Daily Tawar*, a Balochistan-based newspaper.

In September the government signed into law the Prevention of Electronic Crimes Act, 2016, which many critics said contained overly broad and vague definitions of what constituted online speech deemed suitable for removal and/or criminal charges. Digital rights activists expressed serious concerns about the law's potential to curb freedom of expression, particularly on social media. The law states that the government will establish special tribunals for cybercrimes, but it remained unclear how the courts would enforce and interpret the bill.

Additionally, the Electronic Transaction Act and other laws cite a number of offenses involving the misuse of electronic media and systems and the use of such data in other crimes. The act also stipulates that cyberterrorism resulting in a death is punishable by the death penalty or life imprisonment.

The Pakistan Telecommunications Authority (PTA) is responsible for the establishment, operation, and maintenance of telecommunications and has complete control of all content broadcast over telecommunication channels. Despite a 2011 PTA ban on using virtual private networks (VPNs) and voice-over-internet protocol (VOIP), at year's end VPNs and VOIP were both accessible. Many smartphones had built in VPNs. According to Freedom House, two of the best-known services, Spotflux and HotSpot VPN, became inaccessible in January 2014. Spotflux said the government actively blocked its services. The government later restored both.

The government reached an agreement with Google in January to lift its YouTube ban, which had been in place since 2012 after Google declined to remove a controversial video the government considered blasphemous. As part of the agreement, Google set up a localized version of the site, YouTube.pk, which does not include the video.

NGO and internet-freedom observers continued to report that government surveillance online was a concern and that there were indications of the use of surveillance software.

Although internet access and usage was limited, mobile broadband access continued to grow rapidly, reaching 34.3 million subscribers in September. Fixed broadband connections remained very low, at approximately three million subscribers in a population of approximately 199 million.

Academic Freedom and Cultural Events

The government generally did not restrict academic freedom but screened and censored cultural events. At some universities, however, members of student organizations, often with ties to political parties, fostered an atmosphere of intolerance or undue influence that limited the academic freedom of fellow students.

In addition to public schools, there was a large network of madrassahs (private schools run by Muslim clerics) under the supervision of five major governing bodies. These schools varied in their curriculum, with a focus on Islamic texts.

There was government interference with art exhibitions or other musical or cultural activities. The Ministry of Culture operated the Central Board of Film Censors, which previewed and censored sexual content and any content that glorified Indian heroes, leaders, or military figures in foreign and domestic films. In October it banned all Indian content from broadcast in retaliation for a ban on Pakistani artists working on films in India. This ban was lifted on December 17.

b. Freedom of Peaceful Assembly and Association

The constitution and laws provide for the freedoms of assembly and freedom of association, but these freedoms were subject to restrictions.

Freedom of Assembly

By law district authorities may prevent gatherings of more than four persons without police authorization. The law permits the government to ban all rallies and processions, except funeral processions, for security reasons.

Authorities generally prohibited Ahmadis, a religious minority, from holding conferences or gatherings. In December, Punjab provincial police raided the publications department at the Ahmadiyya Muslim Community headquarters in Rabwah and arrested four workers for publishing religious material deemed offensive. According to Ahmadi representatives, the "unprecedented" raid was indicative of worsening conditions for the community in Pakistan.

Several protests, strikes, and demonstrations, both peaceful and violent, took place throughout the country. The government generally prevented political and civil society groups of any affiliation from holding demonstrations in Islamabad, citing security restrictions that limit all public rallies and gatherings in the red-zone section of the city, a secured area where the diplomatic enclave and government buildings are located.

Freedom of Association

The constitution provides for freedom of association subject to certain restrictions imposed by law. The government adopted a series of policies that steadily eroded the freedom of international NGOs (INGOs) to access the communities that they serve. For many project activities, INGOs must request government permission in the form of so-called no-objection certificates (NOCs). INGOs, UN organizations, and international missions have long been required to obtain NOCs before they can conduct most in-country travel or initiate new projects.

In October 2015 the government required that INGOs reregister, a process entailing extensive document requirements, multiple levels of review, and repeated investigations by security and other government offices. As of December more than 60 percent of INGOs that applied for registration under the new system were awaiting a registration decision; none had been rejected. In the meantime the unregistered INGOs ostensibly could not accept new foreign funding or initiate new projects. The government continued to restrict the operating space for the INGOs registered under the new process, delaying or denying visas for some foreign staff or NOCs for official travel.

The government, at both the federal and/or provincial level, similarly restricted the access of local NGOs through NOCs and other requirements. Authorities required NGOs to obtain NOCs before accepting foreign funding, booking hotel or university spaces for events, or working on sensitive human rights issues. Even domestic NGOs with all required NOCs faced government harassment.

c. Freedom of Religion

See the Department of State's *International Religious Freedom Report* at www.state.gov/religiousfreedomreport/.

d. Freedom of Movement, Internally Displaced Persons, Protection of Refugees, and Stateless Persons

The law provides for freedom of internal movement and for uninhibited foreign travel, emigration, and repatriation, but the government limited these rights. The government cooperated with the Office of the UN High Commissioner for Refugees (UNHCR) and other humanitarian organizations in providing protection and assistance to internally displaced persons, refugees, returning refugees, asylum seekers, and other persons of concern.

Abuse of Migrants, Refugees, and Stateless Persons: Pakistan is host to more than 1.3 million Afghan refugees. The government provided temporary legal status to Afghans formally registered and holding Proof of Registration (PoR) cards. In July, the government extended the validity of PoR cards until December 31, and in September, extended the cards an additional three months until March 31, 2017. There were reports, however, of harassment and extortion of Afghan refugees by provincial authorities, police, and host communities. According to UNHCR reports, from January to August, there were 4,150 arrests and detentions, compared with 3,595 for all of 2015. Of those arrested, 99 percent were released, 70 percent without any charges, often following the intervention of UNHCR or its implementing partners. Arrests spiked in August, largely due to security operations and arbitrary actions by the Frontier Corps apprehending Afghans at various checkpoints in Balochistan. There were firsthand accounts of members of the intelligence services harassing refugees. Refugees faced discrimination from local communities. Provincial officials in Khyber Pakhtunkhwa and nationwide cited the presence of Afghan "refugees"--without differentiating between proof of registration (PoR) cardholders, migrants, and temporary visitors--as the cause for deteriorating law and order in major cities. In June the government released press statements that labeled refugee camps safe havens for terrorists and urged the early return of Afghan refugees to their homeland.

In-country Movement: Government restrictions on access to certain areas of FATA, KP, and Balochistan, often due to security concerns, hindered freedom of movement of persons. The government required an approved NOC for travel to areas of the country it designated as "sensitive."

Foreign Travel: The law prohibits travel to Israel, and the country's passports include a statement that they are "valid for all countries except Israel." Passport applicants must list their religious affiliation and, if Muslims, affirm a declaration that the founder of the Ahmadiyya movement was a false prophet. Ahmadi representatives reported the word "Ahmadi" was written on their passports if they refused to sign the declaration. Government employees and students must obtain NOCs from the government before traveling abroad. Authorities rarely enforced this requirement for students.

The government prohibited persons on the Exit Control List from departing the country. The stated purpose of the list was to prevent departure from the country of "persons involved in antistate activities, terrorism, or related to proscribed organizations and those placed on the orders of superior courts." Those on the list had the right to appeal to the courts to have their names removed.

<u>Emigration and Repatriation</u>: During the year the government refused the return of immigrants deported from Europe. One European mission reported several deportees were refused entry as unidentifiable Pakistani citizens despite having passports issued by Pakistani embassies abroad. Some NGOs commented the government increased restrictions on the issuance of identity and proof of nationality documents, such as passports, from its missions abroad.

Internally Displaced Persons

Large population displacements continued as a result of militant activity and military operations in FATA. . The government and UN agencies such as UNHCR and the UN Children's Fund (UNICEF) collaborated to assist and protect those affected by conflict. Once evacuated, internally displaced persons (IDPs) received immunizations, with many of the children receiving them for the first time in five years. The state and relief organizations placed special emphasis on polio, as many IDP children had been vulnerable to the disease due to the Taliban-imposed ban on immunizations in their home regions. In some areas an estimated 50 percent of the IDP population had been displaced five years or longer, according to the Internal Displacement Monitoring Center. Those displaced by conflict generally resided with host families, in rented accommodations, or to a lesser extent, in camps. Several IDP populations settled in informal settlements outside of major cities such as Lahore and Karachi.

The return of IDPs displaced by Operation Zarb-e-Azb in North Waziristan Agency, Operations Khyber I, II, and III in Khyber Agency, and other military activities continued, with 114,511 families returning to FATA and 76,507 families still displaced, according to the UN Office of the Coordinator of Humanitarian Affairs (OCHA). Since 2015, 75 percent of the total IDP population had returned to FATA. OCHA reported that 89 percent of IDPs had returned to Khyber Agency with 9,524 families still displaced; 72 percent had returned to North Waziristan Agency with 29,360 families still displaced; 64 percent had returned to South Waziristan Agency with 23,879 families still displaced; 77 percent had returned to Khurram Agency with 5,457 families still displaced; and 66 percent had returned to Orakzai Agency with 7,965 families still displaced. The average family size in FATA was six. Approximately 16 percent of all returns were female-headed households.

The government required humanitarian organizations assisting civilians displaced by military operations to request NOCs to access all agencies in FATA. According to humanitarian agencies and NGOs, the NOC application process was cumbersome. The government maintained IDP camps inside and near the FATA agencies where military operations took place, despite access and security concerns raised by humanitarian agencies. Humanitarian agency workers providing assistance in the camps were exposed to danger when travelling to and within FATA. UN agencies maintained access to the camps and the affected areas mainly through local NGOs.

There were no reports of involuntary returns. Many IDPs reportedly wanted to return home, despite the lack of local infrastructure, housing, and available service delivery, and the strict control that security forces maintained over returnees' movements via extensive checkpoints. Other IDP families delayed their return or chose some family members to remain in the settled areas of KP where regular access to health care, education, and other social services were available. For IDPs who were unwilling or unable to return, the government coordinated support with UNHCR and other international organizations. The World Food Program distributed food rations to IDPs displaced by conflict and continued to provide rations for extendable periods of six to nine months to IDPs who returned to their areas of origin.

Protection of Refugees

<u>Access to Asylum</u>: The law does not provide for granting asylum or refugee status. The country lacks a legal and regulatory framework for the management of refugees and migration. The law does not exclude asylum seekers and refugees from provisions regarding illegal entry and stay. In the absence of a national refugee legal framework, UNHCR conducted refugee status determination under its mandate, and the country generally accepted UNHCR decisions to grant refugee status and allowed asylum seekers (who were still undergoing the procedure) as

well as recognized refugees to remain in the country pending identification of a durable solution.

Refoulement: In general the government did not forcibly return PoR cardholders, refugees, or asylum seekers to countries where their lives or freedom may be threatened. In August, five PoR cardholders were deported to Afghanistan but were able to return to Pakistan the following day.

Beginning in July there was a sharp increase in UNHCR-assisted returns of PoR cardholders to Afghanistan. In 2015, 58,460 PoR cardholders returned to Afghanistan; between January and June 2016, approximately 8,000 had returned. The returns increased in July, and by early September more than 229,000 Afghan PoR cardholders had returned to Afghanistan. In its emergency funding request, OCHA stated, "The spike in returns is motivated by different factors, including an apparent drastic deterioration of the protection/political space in Pakistan with increasing incidents of detention, forced evictions, police raids, and harassment." Additional factors reported by UNHCR included stricter border management, calls by the Afghan government for refugees to return, harassment and extortion by local authorities and host communities, and the increase of UNHCR's repatriation grant from $200 to $400 per person.

For most of the year, two voluntary repatriation centers operated in Quetta and Peshawar; a third center was opened in Peshawar in September to process the increase in repatriations.

Employment: There is no formal document allowing refugees to work legally, but there is no law prohibiting refugees from working in the country. Many refugees worked as day laborers or in informal markets, and local employers often exploited refugees in the informal labor market with low or unpaid wages. Women and children were particularly vulnerable, accepting underpaid and undesirable work.

Access to Basic Services: One-third of registered Afghans lived in one of 54 refugee villages, while the remaining two-thirds lived in host communities in rural and urban areas and sought to access basic services in those communities. Afghan refugees could avail themselves of the services of police and courts, but some, particularly the poor, were afraid to do so. There were no reports of refugees denied access to a health facility because of their nationality.

The constitution stipulates free and compulsory education for all children between ages five and 16 years regardless of their nationality. Any refugee registered with both UNHCR and the government-run "Commissionerate" of Afghan Refugees was, in theory, admitted to public education facilities after filing the proper paperwork. In practice access to schools was on a space-available basis as determined by the principal, and most registered Afghans attended private Afghan schools or schools sponsored by the international community. For older students, particularly females in refugee villages, access to education remained difficult. Afghans who grew up in Pakistan needed student visas to attend universities, but they qualified for student visas based on their PoR cards. Afghan students were eligible to seek admission to Pakistani public and private colleges and universities. In public statements, including at the Leadership Summit on Refugees on September 20, the government reaffirmed the right of all children, regardless of status, to public primary education.

Durable Solutions: The government did not accept refugees for resettlement from other countries and did not facilitate local integration. The government does not accord Afghan refugees Pakistani citizenship.

Stateless Persons

Statelessness continued to be a problem. There is no national legislation on statelessness, and the government does not recognize the existence of stateless persons. International and national agencies estimated there were possibly thousands of stateless persons as a result of the 1947 and 1971 partitions of India and Pakistan, and of Pakistan and Bangladesh, respectively.

Section 3. Freedom to Participate in the Political Process

The constitution provides the majority of citizens the ability to choose their government in free and fair periodic elections held by secret ballot and based on universal and equal suffrage. Gilgit-Baltistan, AJK, FATA, and PATA) have political systems that differ from the rest of the country. FATA and PATA had representation in the national Parliament; Gilgit-Baltistan and AJK did not.

Despite their representation in the national Parliament, FATA residents do not have a voice in federal decisions regarding the tribal areas; authority in FATA resides with the president. Tribal residents do not have the right to change their local government, because unelected civilian bureaucrats nominally run the tribal agencies under the 1901 FCR, as amended in 2011. No local government elections were held in FATA, even as the country's other provinces elected local representatives. Through the 2011 Extension of the Political Parties Order 2002 to the Tribal Areas, the government allowed political parties to operate freely in FATA. Political observers credited this order with laying the foundation for a more mature political system in the tribal agencies, and there was ongoing internal debate over the possibility of FATA's integration into KP Province to normalize its administration. In December 2016 the Committee on FATA reforms, established by Prime Minister Sharif, formally recommended that FATA be merged with KP Province.

AJK has an interim constitution, an elected unicameral assembly, a prime minister, and a president elected by the assembly. During the year AJK held legislative assembly elections that resulted in a PML-N-majority government. Media reported that local observers concluded the elections were largely peaceful and free of allegations of vote rigging; the AJK election commission deployed an additional 32,000 law enforcement officers to maintain law and order. Some AJK political leaders reported an increased military presence on election day. The federal government, including the military, controlled and influenced the structures of the AJK government and its electoral politics. Authorities barred those who did not support AJK's accession to Pakistan from the political process, government employment, and educational institutions.

Elections and Political Participation

<u>Recent Elections</u>: In 2013 the country held national elections that resulted in a PML-N-majority government led by Prime Minister Nawaz Sharif. In 2013 Mamnoon Hussain succeeded Asif Ali Zardari as president.

For the 2013 elections, the Election Commission of Pakistan (ECP) accredited approximately 43,000 domestic observers, the majority of whom were from the Free and Fair Election Network. The EU, Democracy International, the Aurat Foundation, and the National Democratic Institute were among the many groups that observed the election. The government permitted all existing political parties to contest the elections. Although several boycotted, the largest parties participated. Election observers generally considered the elections a success, despite terrorist violence and some procedural problems.

The International Foundation for Electoral Systems noted weak formal adjudication of challenges of disputed election results and also the high courts' failure to meet statutorily prescribed deadlines for adjudication in the majority of cases.

As a result of alleged irregularities in balloting and in the candidates' documentation during the 2013 elections, election tribunals constituted by the ECP removed legislators from three constituencies in Punjab from office, including the speaker of the National Assembly and the minister of railways. The tribunals ordered that by-elections or repolling be conducted in all three constituencies.

<u>Political Parties and Political Participation</u>: There were few restrictions on political parties. In most areas there was no interference with the rights to organize, run for election, seek votes, or publicize views. In Balochistan, however, there were reports security agencies and separatist groups harassed local political parties, such as the Balochistan National Party and the Balochistan Student Organization.

<u>Participation of Women and Minorities</u>: While no laws prevent women from voting, cultural and traditional barriers in tribal and rural areas impeded some women from voting. Authorities widely used quotas to assure a minimum female presence in elected bodies. There are 60 seats in the National Assembly reserved for women. Authorities apportioned these seats on the basis of total votes secured by the candidates of each political party that contested the elections. Authorities reserved 129 of the 758 seats in provincial assemblies and one-third of the seats in local councils for women. Women participated actively as political party members, but they were not always successful in securing leadership positions within parties, with the exception of women's wings. Women served in the federal cabinet.

The government requires voters to indicate their religion when registering to vote and requires Ahmadis to declare themselves as non-Muslims. Since Ahmadis consider themselves Muslims, many were unable to vote if they did not comply.

The constitution reserves four seats in the Senate, one for each of the four provinces, for religious minorities, defined by the government as "non-Muslim." These seats are filled through indirect elections held in the provincial assemblies. Ten National Assembly seats are reserved for members of religious minorities. The authorities apportioned seats to parties based on the percentage of seats each won in the assembly. Minorities held 23 reserved seats in the provincial assemblies: eight in Punjab, nine in Sindh, three in KP, and three in Balochistan.

Women and minorities may contest unreserved seats.

Section 4. Corruption and Lack of Transparency in Government

The law provides criminal penalties for official corruption, but the government did not implement the law effectively, and officials frequently engaged in corrupt practices. Corruption was pervasive in politics and government, and various politicians and public office holders faced allegations of corruption, including bribery, extortion, cronyism, nepotism, patronage, graft, and embezzlement.

Corruption: Corruption within the lower levels of police was common. Some police charged fees to register genuine complaints and accepted bribes for registering false complaints. Bribes to avoid charges were commonplace.

Anecdotal reports persisted about corruption in the judicial system, including reports of small-scale facilitation payments requested by court staff. Lower courts reportedly remained corrupt, inefficient, and subject to pressure from higher-ranking judges as well as prominent, wealthy, religious, and political figures.

The NAB serves as the highest-level anticorruption organization, with a mandate to eliminate corruption through awareness, prevention, and enforcement. The NAB and other investigative agencies, including the Federal Board of Revenue, State Bank of Pakistan and the Federal Investigative Authority, were reportedly opening investigations into corruption, tax evasion, and money laundering following international press reports of Pakistanis named in the "Panama Papers" and "Bahamas Leaks" revelations of offshore banking accounts from the International Consortium of Investigative Journalists. In November the Supreme Court convened a special bench to investigate allegations of corruption levelled against the prime minister and members of his family. After several sessions in November and December, the Supreme Court adjourned without issuing a judgment. The case was scheduled to be taken up by a new bench in early 2017.

The director general of KP's Accountability (Ehtesab) Commission resigned in February, alleging that amendments to the province's accountability legislation had compromised the commission's autonomy and rendered his position redundant. The director of the province's Anti-Corruption Establishment (which likewise investigates corruption cases) was transferred from his post in May and faced an inquiry regarding the investigations he led.

Financial Disclosure: There are many laws regarding the disclosure of assets and liabilities of civil servants and elected officials. By law members of parliament, civil servants, and ministers must declare their assets. Failure to disclose this information may lead to their disqualification from public office for 10 years.

Heads of state, in contrast, are not required to declare their income and assets. The assets of judges, generals, and high-level officials were often concealed from the public.

Under the Efficiency and Disciplinary Rules, an official must face an inquiry if accused of corruption or financial irregularities. If the inquiry results in a derogatory finding, the accused official faces criminal charges. A person convicted of corruption faces a prison term of up to 14 years, a fine, or both. The government may appropriate any money, property, or other assets obtained by corrupt means.

Political parties and politicians must file annual financial accounting reports declaring their assets and liabilities. The law was not fully implemented, and lawmakers often disregarded it. It is the duty of the ECP to verify that political parties and politicians make their financial information publicly available; the ECP posted the list of parliamentarians' assets in January.

Public Access to Information: The law allows any citizen access to public records held by a public body of the federal government, including ministries, departments, boards, councils, courts, and tribunals. It does not apply to government-owned corporations or provincial governments. Bodies subject to the law must respond to requests for access within 21 days. Regulations restrict certain records from public access, including classified documents, those deemed harmful to a law enforcement case or an individual, or those that would cause grave and significant damage to the economy or the interests of the nation. NGOs criticized the law for having too many exempt categories and for not encouraging proactive disclosure. KP and Punjab provincial governments enacted provincial Right To Information laws.

Section 5. Governmental Attitude Regarding International and Nongovernmental Investigation of Alleged Violations of Human Rights

A variety of domestic and international human rights groups generally operated without government restriction, investigating and publishing their findings on human rights cases. Some groups that implicated the government, or the military or intelligence services, in misdeeds or worked on issues related to IDPs and areas of conflict reported their operations were at times restricted. Very few NGOs had access to KP, FATA, and certain areas in Balochistan. International staff members of organizations faced delays in the issuance of visas and NOCs for in-country travel.

The government also released new guidance for INGOs (see section 2.b.). Some civil society actors expressed concern the language could be misused to restrict legitimate work such as governance support or human rights advocacy. There were no reports that the government found an INGO in violation of this regulation.

The government increasingly restricted the operating space of domestic and international human rights groups, particularly those that work on issues related to government abuses, IDPs, conflict areas, and advocacy. These groups faced numerous regulations regarding travel, visas, and registration that hampered their ability to program and fundraise. International staff members of organizations, including those from the few successfully registered INGOs, continued to face delays in the issuance of visas and NOCs for in-country travel.

The new INGO registration regulations announced in October 2015 prohibits INGOs from participating in "political activities" and "antistate activities," but the regulations neither define these terms nor indicate what body would be responsible for adjudicating claims against INGOs.

Security threats were a problem for NGO workers, and organizations that promoted women's rights faced particular challenges.

Government Human Rights Bodies: The Senate and National Assembly Standing Committees on Law, Justice, Minorities, and Human Rights held hearings on a range of human rights problems, including honor crimes, police abuses in connection with the blasphemy law, and the Hudood Ordinance. The committees served as useful forums in which to raise public awareness of such problems, but their conclusions generally adhered to existing government policy. The committees did little beyond broad oversight. The 2012 National Commission for Human Rights Bill authorized the establishment of an independent committee, the National Commission on Human Rights, and the government constituted the commission in 2015. An independent Ministry of Human Rights was reconstituted in November 2015.

Section 6. Discrimination, Societal Abuses, and Trafficking in Persons

Women

Rape and Domestic Violence: Rape is a criminal offense, with punishment that ranges from a minimum of 10 to 25 years in prison and a fine to the death penalty.

The penalty for gang rape is death or life imprisonment, but sentences, when convictions occurred, were often less severe. Although rape was frequent, prosecutions were rare. According to data presented by the Ministry of Interior to the senate in 2014, there had been no rape convictions in the country during previous years. Spousal rape is not a crime. During the year Parliament passed a new antirape law that provides for collection of DNA evidence and includes nondisclosure of a rape victim's name, the right to legal representation of rape victims, and enhanced penalties for rape of victims with mental or physical disabilities.

As in previous years, the government did not effectively enforce the 2006 Women's Protection Act. The act brought the crime of rape under the jurisdiction of criminal rather than Islamic courts. By law police are not allowed to arrest or hold a female victim overnight at a police station without a civil court judge's consent. The law requires a victim to complain directly to a sessions court, which is considered a trial court for heinous offenses. After recording the victim's statement, the sessions court judge officially lodges a complaint, after which police may then make arrests. NGOs reported the procedure created barriers for rape victims who could not afford to travel to or access the courts. Rape was a severely underreported crime.

The provincial government of Punjab passed the Punjab Protection of Women Against Violence Act (2016) in February to provide greater legal protections for domestic abuse victims, including judicial protective orders and access to a new network of district-level women's shelters, the first of which was scheduled to open in Multan.

There were no reliable national, provincial, or local statistics on rape due to underreporting and a lack of any centralized law enforcement data collection system.

According to the Aurat Foundation and others, prosecutions of reported rapes were rare. Police and NGOs reported individuals involved in other types of disputes sometimes filed false rape charges, reducing the ability of police to identify legitimate cases and proceed with prosecution. NGOs reported police were at times implicated in rape cases. NGOs also alleged police sometimes abused or threatened victims, demanding they drop charges, especially when police received bribes from suspected perpetrators or the perpetrators were influential community leaders. Some police demanded bribes from victims before registering rape charges, and investigations were sometimes superficial. The use of postrape medical testing increased, but medical personnel in many areas did not have sufficient training or equipment, which further complicated prosecutions. Accusations of rape were often resolved using extrajudicial measures, with the victim often forced to marry her attacker.

No specific federal law prohibits domestic violence, which was widespread. Husbands reportedly beat and occasionally killed their wives. Other forms of domestic violence included torture, physical disfigurement, and shaving the eyebrows and hair off women's heads. In-laws abused and harassed the wives of their sons. Dowry and other family-related disputes sometimes resulted in death or disfigurement by burning or acid.

Women who tried to report abuse faced serious challenges. Police and judges were sometimes reluctant to take action in domestic violence cases, viewing them as family problems. Instead of filing charges, police typically responded by encouraging the parties to reconcile. Authorities routinely returned abused women to their abusive family members.

To address societal norms that disapprove of victims who report gender-based violence and abuse, the government established women's police stations, staffed by female officers, to offer women a safe haven where they could safely report complaints and file charges. Men were also able to use these police stations. These women's police stations, however, struggled with understaffing and limited equipment. Training female police and changing the cultural assumptions of male police also remained challenges. Due to restrictions on women's mobility and social pressures related to women's appearance in public, utilization of women's police centers was limited, but NGOs and officials reported that use was growing and more centers were needed. Many women remained unaware of the centers.

The government continued to operate the Crisis Center for Women in Distress, which referred abused women to NGOs for assistance. Twenty-six government-funded Shaheed Benazir Bhutto Centers for Women across the country provided legal aid, medical treatment, and psychosocial counseling. These centers served women who were victims of exploitation and violence. Victims later were referred to "Dar-ul-Amans," or shelter houses, and funds from provincial Women Development Departments had established approximately 200 such homes for abused women and children. These provided shelter and access to medical treatment. According to NGOs the shelters did not offer other assistance to women, such as legal aid or counseling, and primarily served as halfway homes for women awaiting trial for adultery, even though they were the victims of rape and domestic abuse.

Government centers lacked sufficient space, staff, and resources. Conditions in the Dar-ul-Amans did not meet international standards. They were severely overcrowded with, in some cases, more than 35 women sharing one toilet. Few shelters offered access to basic needs such as showers, laundry supplies, or feminine hygiene products. Some shelters were given a daily food allowance of nine rupees ($0.09) to feed nearly 100 women.

There were some reports of women being trafficked and prostituted out of shelters. Shelter staff reportedly sometimes discriminated against women in shelters; they assumed that if women fled their homes, it was because they were women of ill repute. In some cases women were reportedly abused at the government-run shelters, found their movements severely restricted, or were pressured to return to their abusers.

Female Genital Mutilation/Cutting (FGM/C): No national law addresses the practice of FGM/C. According to human rights groups and media reports, between 70 and 90 percent of Dawoodi Bohra Muslims practiced various forms of FGM/C, often in private homes and without medical supervision. A population of approximately 40,000 Dawoodi Bohra Muslims lived in Karachi, with smaller pockets in Lahore, Islamabad, and other cities. Some Dawoodi Bohras spoke publicly and signed online petitions against the practice. Some isolated tribes and communities in rural Sindh and Balochistan also practiced FGM/C.

Other Harmful Traditional Practices: At times women were victims of various types of societal violence and abuse, including so-called honor killings, forced marriages, imposed isolation, and being used as chattel to settle tribal disputes. There were cases in which husbands and male family members treated women as chattel.

A 2004 law on honor killings and the 2011 Prevention of Anti-Women Practices Act already criminalize acts committed against women in the name of traditional practices. Despite these laws hundreds of women reportedly were victims of honor killings. Many cases went unreported and unpunished. The practice of "karo-kari" or "siyah kari"--a premeditated honor killing that occurs if a family, community, tribal court, or jirga determines that adultery or some other "crime of honor" occurred--continued across the country. Karo-kari derives from "black male" (karo) and "black female" (kari), metaphoric terms for someone who has dishonored the family or is an adulterer or adulteress. In many cases the male involved in the alleged "crime of honor" is not killed but allowed to flee. In October the government passed the antihonor killing law, closing the loophole that allowed perpetrators in "honor killings" to go free so as long as the victim's family pardoned the perpetrator.

Police in Sindh established karo-kari cells with a free telephone number in the districts of Sukkur, Ghotki, Khairpur, and Nausharo Feroze for persons to report karo-kari incidents. Because honor crimes generally occurred within families, many went unreported. Police and NGOs reported that increased media coverage enabled law enforcement officials to take some action against a limited number of perpetrators. In July social media celebrity Qandeel Baloch was killed by her brother at their family home in southern Punjab. The brother said his sister had shamed the family with her "liberal" lifestyle and for posing in photographs with a famous mullah. The government charged Baloch's brother and accomplices with her murder and invoked Section 311 of the penal code, which made the state a party against the brother. This effectively barred the family from "forgiving" the brother and setting him free, a common outcome in these types of murders.

The practice of cutting off a woman's nose or ears, especially in connection with honor crimes, was reported, but legal repercussions were rare.

Although prohibited by law, the practice of buying and selling brides also continued in rural areas. Many tribes, communities, or families practiced sequestering women from all contact with men other than their relatives. Despite prohibitions on handing over women as compensation for crimes or as a resolution of a dispute (also known as "vani" or "swara"), the practice continued in Punjab and KP. In rural Sindh landowning families continued the practice of "marriage to the Quran," forcing a female family member to stay unmarried to avoid division of property. Property of women "married to the Quran" remained under the legal control of their fathers or eldest brothers, and such women were prohibited from contact with any man older than age 14. Families expected these women to stay in the home and not contact anyone outside their families.

In February the Sindh Assembly approved the Hindu Marriage Act, which creates a specific legal mechanism to register Hindu marriages and to prove the legitimacy of marriages under the law. Observers viewed these new bills as the step forward in protecting Hindu minorities, particularly Hindu women who are disproportionately targeted for abductions and forced conversions. One controversial provision of the Sindh law provides that a marriage between Hindus is to be dissolved if either party converts to a different religion; some members of Hindu communities worried this provision could be used to break up marriages by forcing women to convert to Islam, which would then nullify the marriage and permit the women to marry Muslim men.

The 2011 Prevention of Anti-Women Practices Amendment Act criminalizes and punishes giving a woman in marriage to settle a civil or criminal dispute; depriving a woman of her rights to inherit movable or immovable property by deceitful or illegal means; coercing or in any manner compelling a woman to enter into marriage; and compelling, arranging, or facilitating the marriage of a woman with the Quran, including forcing her to take an oath on the Quran to remain unmarried or not to claim her share of an inheritance.

The 2010 Acid Control and Acid Crime Practice Bill makes maiming or killing via corrosive substance a crime and imposes stiff penalties against perpetrators. As with other laws, these measures are not applicable in FATA and PATA unless the president issues a notification to that effect. Nevertheless, there were numerous acid attacks on women across the country, with few perpetrators bought to justice. In July media reported that a spurned suitor threw acid at the family who rejected his marriage proposal, injuring six individuals.

The 2012 National Commission on the Status of Women Bill provides for the commission's financial and administrative autonomy to investigate violations of women's rights. According to women's rights activists, however, the commission lacked resources and remained powerless. The position of the commission's chairperson remained vacant for most of the year.

Sexual Harassment: Although the 2010 Criminal Law Amendment Act and the Protection Against Harassment of Women at Workplace Act criminalize sexual harassment in the workplace and public sphere, the problem was widespread. The law requires all provinces to establish provincial-level ombudsmen. Sindh was the first province to do so, in 2012. Punjab Province and administrative district Gilgit-Baltistan also established ombudsmen. Neither Balochistan nor KP had an ombudsman. Press reports indicated harassment was especially high among domestic workers and nurses. According to press reports, some women were harassed via social media. In August police charged a man in Nowshera, KP, with online harassment under the recently passed cybercrimes legislation.

Reproductive Rights: Couples and individuals have the right to decide the number, spacing, and timing of children, but they often lacked the information and means to do so. Young girls and women were especially vulnerable to problems related to sexual and reproductive health and reproductive rights. They often lacked information and means to access care. According to a survey by the Women's Empowerment Group released in 2013, only 25 percent of adolescents were aware of their sexual and reproductive rights. Spousal opposition also contributed to the challenges women faced in obtaining contraception or delaying pregnancy. According to UN Population Division estimates in 2016, 29 percent of women of reproductive age used a modern method of contraception. Access by women, particularly in rural areas, to health and reproductive rights education remained difficult due to social constraints. For these same reasons, data collection was also difficult.

According to the National Institute of Population Studies' *2012-13 Demographic and Health Survey*, 27 percent of women received no prenatal care; however, the report showed a substantial improvement in the proportion of mothers receiving antenatal care over the prior 13 years, increasing from 43 percent in 2001 to 73 percent in 2013. The survey also revealed that skilled health-care providers delivered 52 percent of births and that 48 percent of births took place in a medical facility.

According to the most recent UN research, the maternal mortality ratio was 178 deaths per 100,000 live births, a rate attributed to lack of health information and services. Few women in rural areas had access to skilled attendants during childbirth, including essential obstetric and postpartum care. According to UNICEF, deteriorating security caused displacement and affected access to medical services, especially in KP and FATA.

Discrimination: Women faced legal and economic discrimination. The law prohibits discrimination on the basis of sex in general, but authorities did not enforce it. Also, women faced discrimination in family law, property law, and the judicial system. Family law formulates protection for women in cases of divorce, including requirements for maintenance, and sets clear guidelines for custody of minor children and their maintenance. Many women were unaware of these legal protections or unable to obtain legal counsel to enforce them. Divorced women often were left with no means of support, as their families ostracized them. Women are legally free to marry without family consent, but society frequently ostracized women who did so, or they risked becoming victims of honor crimes.

The 2011 Prevention of Anti-Women Practices Act makes it illegal to deny women inheritance of property by deceitful means. The law entitles female children to one-half the inheritance of male children. Wives inherit one-eighth of their husband's estate. Women often received far less than their legal entitlement. Women faced significant discrimination in employment and frequently were paid less than men for similar work.

Children

Birth Registration: Citizenship is derived by birth in the country, although for children born abroad after 2000, citizenship may be derived by descent if either the mother or the father is a citizen and the child is registered with the proper authorities (see section 2.d.). Reporting of births is voluntary, and records are not kept uniformly, particularly in rural areas. While the government reported that it registered more than 75 percent of the population, observers believed actual figures were lower. Public services, such as education and health care, were available to children without a birth certificate.

Education: The constitution mandates compulsory education provided free by the government to all children between the ages of five and 16. Government schools often charged parents for books, uniforms, and other materials. Parents of lower economic means sometimes chose to send children to madrassahs, where they received free room and board, or to NGO-operated schools.

The most significant barrier to girls' education was the lack of access. Public schools, particularly beyond the primary grades, were not available in many rural areas, and those that existed were often too far for a girl to travel unaccompanied. Despite cultural beliefs that boys and girls should be educated separately after primary school, the government often failed to take measures to provide separate restroom facilities or separate classrooms, and there were more government schools for boys than for girls. The attendance rates for girls in primary, secondary, and postsecondary schools were lower than for boys. Additionally, certain tribal and cultural beliefs often prevented girls from attending schools.

Medical Care: Boys and girls had equal access to government facilities, although families were more likely to seek medical assistance for boys than girls.

Child Abuse: Child abuse was widespread. Employers, who in some cases were relatives, abused young girls and boys working as domestic servants by beating them and forcing them to work long hours. Many such children were trafficking victims. While there was no official count of street children, SPARC estimated they numbered 1.5 million.

Local authorities subjected children to harmful traditional practices such as "swara," treating girls as chattel to settle disputes and debts.

In February the government updated its definition of statutory rape and expanded the previous definition, which was sexual intercourse with a girl younger than age 16, to include boys.

Early and Forced Marriage: Despite legal prohibitions, child marriages occurred. The law sets the legal age of marriage at 18 for men and 16 for women and prescribes punishment for violators of imprisonment for up to a month, a fine of 1,000 rupees ($9.90), or both.

In 2014 the Council of Islamic Ideology declared the marriage laws to be un-Islamic and noted they were "unfair and there cannot be any legal age of marriage." The council stated that Islam does not prohibit underage marriage since it allows the consummation of marriage after both partners reach puberty. Decisions of the Council are non-binding.

Many young girls and women were victims of forced marriages arranged by their families. Although forced marriage is a criminal offense and many cases were filed, prosecution remained a problem. In 2012 the Family Planning Association of Pakistan estimated that child marriages constituted 30 percent of marriages. In rural areas poor parents sometimes sold their daughters into marriage, in some cases to settle debts or disputes.

In 2013 Sindh passed the Child Marriage Restraint Act, which criminalizes marriages to children under the age of 16. Despite this legislation Sindh had not effectively stopped the practice of early child marriage. In March, three men were arrested under the act after one of the men married a 15-year-old girl. In June a 61-year-old man was arrested for marrying an 11-year-old girl in Jacobabad district. The Punjab provincial assembly passed a law in March 2015 increasing the penalties for parents and clerics who assisted in marriages between children, although the law left the legal minimum age for women to marry at 16.

Female Genital Mutilation/Cutting: Information on FGM/C is provided in the women's section above.

Sexual Exploitation of Children: In March, Parliament amended the criminal code to protect further children from specific crimes of child pornography, sexual abuse, seduction, and cruelty. The 1961 Suppression of Prostitution Ordinance and portions of the penal code are intended to protect children from sexual exploitation. Authorities did not regularly enforce these laws. Child pornography is illegal under obscenity laws. Socioeconomic vulnerabilities led to the sexual exploitation of children, including trafficking for sexual exploitation. Many children, including trafficking victims forced to beg at bus terminals and on the side of the road, experienced sexual and physical abuse. In May a sex abuse scandal involving the kidnapping, drugging, sexual abuse, and filming of young boys for child pornography by a gang in Swat was reported by media and civil society; however, the March amendment to the criminal code was reportedly not applicable to PATA, FATA, Gilgit-Baltistan, and AJK.

Infanticide or Infanticide of Children with Disabilities: By law anyone found to have abandoned an infant may be jailed for seven years, while anyone guilty of secretly burying a deceased child may be imprisoned for two years. Murder is punishable by life imprisonment, but authorities rarely prosecuted the crime of infanticide.

Displaced Children: According to civil society sources, it was difficult for children displaced by military operations to access education or psychological support. SPARC and other child rights organizations expressed concern that children displaced by flooding and conflict were vulnerable to child labor abuses as some families relocated to urban areas. Doctors working in IDP camps reported difficulty in treating the large influx of patients, including children and elderly persons, because they were especially sensitive to disease, malnutrition, and other unhealthy conditions. Poor hygiene and crowded conditions found in the IDP communities caused some children to contract skin rashes, gastroenteritis, and respiratory infections. The government provided polio vaccinations to many displaced children who were not inoculated, since they came from areas where militant groups banned vaccination campaigns (see section 2.d.).

International Child Abductions: The country is not a party to the 1980 Hague Convention on the Civil Aspects of International Child Abduction. See the Department of State's *Annual Report on International Parental Child Abduction* at travel.state.gov/content/childabduction/en/legal/compliance.html.

Anti-Semitism

There is a very small Jewish population in the country. Anti-Semitic sentiments were widespread in the vernacular press. Hate speech broadcast by traditional media and through social media derogatorily used terms such as "Jewish agent" and "Yahoodi" to attack individuals and groups.

Trafficking in Persons

See the Department of State's *Trafficking in Persons Report* at www.state.gov/j/tip/rls/tiprpt/.

Persons with Disabilities

The law provides for equal rights for of persons with disabilities, but authorities did not always implement its provisions. After the Ministry of Social Welfare and Special Education was dissolved in 2011, its affiliated departments--including the Directorate General for Special Education, National Council for the Rehabilitation of the Disabled, and National Trust for the Disabled--were transferred to the Capital Administration and Development Division. The special education and social welfare offices, which devolved to the provinces, are responsible for protecting the rights of persons with disabilities.

In the provinces social welfare departments worked for the welfare and education of persons with disabilities. In Sindh the law mandates the minister for bonded labor and special education to address the educational needs of persons with disabilities. According to civil society sources, most children with disabilities did not attend school. At the higher-education level, Allama Iqbal Open University, the University of the Punjab, and Karachi University had programs to train students as educators for individuals with disabilities.

The government's 2003 National Disability Policy designated the federal capital and provincial capitals as disability-friendly cities and granted permission to persons with disabilities to take central superior service exams to compete for entry to the civil service. The policy also provided for 127 special education centers in main cities. Employment quotas at the federal and provincial levels require public and private organizations to reserve at least 2 percent of jobs for qualified persons with disabilities. Authorities only partially implemented this requirement due to lack of adequate enforcement mechanisms. In Lahore, beginning in 2014 and continuing sporadically thereafter, persons with vision disabilities held protests against the lack of jobs, which were in short supply despite the legal quota. Families cared for most individuals with physical and mental disabilities.

Organizations that did not wish to hire persons with disabilities could instead pay a fine to a disability assistance fund. Authorities rarely enforced this obligation. The National Council for the Rehabilitation of the Disabled provided job placement and loan facilities, as well as subsistence funding. There were no legal restrictions on the rights of persons with disabilities to vote or participate in civil affairs. Voting was challenging for persons with disabilities, however, because of severe difficulties in obtaining transportation and access to polling stations.

Acts of Violence, Discrimination, and Other Abuses Based on Sexual Orientation and Gender Identity

Consensual same-sex sexual conduct is a criminal offense; however, the government rarely prosecuted cases. The penalty for same-sex relations is a fine, two years' to life imprisonment, or both. Lesbian, gay, bisexual, transgender, and intersex (LGBTI) persons rarely revealed their sexual orientation or gender identity. No laws protect against discrimination on the basis of sexual orientation or gender identity. Discrimination against LGBTI persons was widely acknowledged privately, but insufficient data existed for accurate reporting, due in part to severe societal stigma and fear of recrimination on the part of any who came forward. In 2013 the Pakistan Telecommunications Authority blocked the country's first online platform for the LGBTI community to share views and network, but social media pages working on LGBTI rights and related issues continued to function.

Violence and discrimination continued against LGBTI persons. Police generally refused to take action on cases involving members of the LGBTI community. In November a gang of 20 men in Sialkot assaulted and physically abused five transgender women. After a video of the attack appeared online and the transgender community protested, police arrested members of the gang. In April a transgender woman received delayed medical treatment in Peshawar following multiple gunshot wounds and later succumbed to her injuries. The provincial government launched an investigation against the hospital administration that refused to treat her and police officials who allegedly would not file charges against them. In July, three transgender women reportedly were raped in Faisalabad.

Society generally shunned transgender persons, eunuchs, and intersex persons, collectively referred to as "hijras," who often lived together in slum communities and survived by begging and dancing at carnivals and weddings. Some also were prostitutes. Local authorities often denied hijras places in schools or admission to hospitals, and landlords often refused to rent or sell property to them. Authorities often denied hijras their share of inherited property. A 2012 Supreme Court ruling recognizes hijras as a "third gender" and allows them to obtain accurate national identification cards. Because of the ruling, hijras fully participated in the 2013 elections for the first time as candidates and voters. In June a group of muftis (religious leaders) issued a fatwa (religious ruling) that allows transgender persons to marry other transgenders.

HIV and AIDS Social Stigma

Societal attitudes toward HIV-positive individuals were changing, but discrimination persisted. Cases of discrimination often went unreported due to the stigma faced by HIV/AIDS patients. In addition to operating treatment centers, the National Aids Control Program held rallies and public campaigns and spoke in mosques about birth control and AIDS awareness. The government established 13 HIV treatment and care centers nationwide, which provided comprehensive HIV-care services.

Other Societal Violence or Discrimination

Societal violence due to religious intolerance remained a serious problem. Occasionally, there were reports of mob violence against religious minorities, including Christians, Ahmadiyya Muslims, Hindus, and Shia Muslims. In July rioting occurred in Mehrab Samejo in Sindh's Ghotki district after an incident in which a previously Hindu convert to Islam was accused of desecrating the Quran. Two Hindu men were subsequently shot during a mob attack.

In late June a mob of local residents clashed with members of the small Kalash tribe in Chitral after a teenage Kalash girl alleged that she was forced to convert to Islam; the Kalash people are adherent to pre-Islamic beliefs. Local law enforcement responded quickly and dispersed the mob; some minor injuries to Kalash villagers in the Bumburate valley were recorded.

Members of the Hazara ethnic minority, who are Shia Muslim, continued to face discrimination and threats of violence in Quetta, Balochistan. According to press reports and other sources, they were unable to move freely outside of Quetta's two Hazara-populated enclaves. Consumer goods in those enclaves were available only at inflated prices, and Hazaras reported an inability to find employment or pursue higher education. They also alleged government agencies discriminated against Hazaras in issuing identification cards and passports. To avoid causing violent incidents, authorities confined Shia religious processions to the Hazara enclaves. Anti-Shia graffiti was common in Quetta. According to press reports, there were several attacks on Hazaras during the year. Media reported that three Hazaras were killed and nine others injured in separate attacks in Quetta in May. In June, five Harazas were killed in Quetta. Two Hazara men were shot in Quetta on August 1.

Section 7. Worker Rights

a. Freedom of Association and the Right to Collective Bargaining

The vast majority of the labor force was under the jurisdiction of provincial labor laws. A 2010 constitutional amendment, which devolved labor legislation and policies to the four provinces, stipulated that existing national laws would remain in force "until altered, repealed, or amended" by the provincial governments. Provinces implemented their own industrial relations acts in 2011. In 2012 Parliament passed a new industrial relations act that took International Labor Organization (ILO) conventions into account but applied them only to the Islamabad Capital Territory and to trade federations that operated in more than one province. Most of the labor force was not covered by federal labor regulations of any kind.

The role of the federal government remained unclear in the wake of devolution. The only federal government body with any authority over labor issues was the Ministry of Human Resource, Development, and Overseas Pakistanis, whose role was limited to compiling statistics to demonstrate compliance with ILO conventions. At the provincial level, laws providing for collective bargaining rights excluded banking and financial sector workers, forestry workers, hospital workers, self-employed farmers, and persons employed in an administrative capacity or managerial capacity.

Without any federal-level legislation or federal-level entity responsible for labor, the continued existence of the National Industrial Relations Commission remained in question. The 2012 federal industrial relations act stipulates that the commission may adjudicate and determine industrial disputes within the Islamabad Capital Territory to which a trade union/federation of trade unions is a party and any other industrial dispute determined by the government to be of national importance. This provision does not provide a forum specifically for interprovincial disputes but appears to allow for the possibility that the commission could resolve such a dispute.

Worker organizations noted the limited capacity and funding for labor relations implementation at the provincial level, and there was controversy over the federal government's decision to maintain control of the Workers Welfare Fund and Employees Old Age Benefits Institution as opposed to devolving it to the provinces.

The law prohibited state administrators, government and state enterprises, workers in export processing zones, and public-sector workers from collective bargaining and striking, but labor groups reported the law was not applied during the year. The provincial industrial relations acts also address and limit strikes and lockouts. For example, the KP act specifies that when a "strike or lockout lasts for more than 30 days, the government may, by order in writing, prohibit the strike or lockout" and must then refer the dispute to a labor court.

Unions were able to organize large-scale strikes, but police often broke up the strikes, and employers used them to justify dismissals. Marches and protests also occurred regularly, although police often arrested union leaders and occasionally charged them under antiterrorism and antistate laws. Violence and other problems involving freedom of association persisted throughout the year.

Federal law defines illegal strikes, picketing, and other types of protests as "civil commotion," which carries a penalty of up to life imprisonment. The law also states that gatherings of four or more persons may require police authorization, a provision authorities could use against trade union gatherings, since the federal government has authority on criminal matters.

The passage of the 18th amendment to the constitution dissolved the federal Ministry of Labor and Manpower, resulting in the devolution of labor issues to the provinces. Labor groups, international organizations, and NGOs remained critical of the devolution, contending that certain labor issues--including minimum wages, worker rights, national labor standards, and observance of international labor conventions--should remain within the purview of the federal government. Observers also raised concerns about the provinces' varying capacity and commitment to adopt and enforce labor laws. Some international organizations observed the devolution gave responsibility to the provincial authorities, and they noticed some improvements in labor practices, including inspections.

In July the government of Punjab passed the Punjab Restriction on Employment of Children Ordinance, 2016, which includes provisions aimed at protecting children from labor exploitation. Other provinces also passed legislation during the year on child labor and child protection, and all four provinces dedicated resources to address child labor practices.

Labor leaders also stressed the need for legislation to cover the rights of workers in the informal and agricultural sectors. The majority of factory workers were employed as contract labor with no benefits beyond basic wages and no long-term job security, even if they remained with the same employer for years. Factory managers were often unable to ascertain the identity of fire or other work-related accident victims because these individuals generally did not appear in official records. In August a shop roof collapsed in Lahore, injuring five workers. According to media reports, the roof collapsed due to disrepair. In November an undetermined amount of workers (some reportedly undocumented) died in an explosion and fire at a ship-breaking facility in Gadani, Sindh Province.

Enforcement of labor laws remained weak, in large part due to lack of resources and political will. Most unions functioned independently of government and political party influence. Labor leaders raised concerns about employers sponsoring management-friendly or only-on-paper worker unions, so-called yellow unions, to prevent effective unionization.

There were no reported cases of the government dissolving a union without due process. Unions could be administratively "deregistered," however, without judicial review.

Labor NGOs assisted workers by providing technical training and capacity-building workshops to strengthen labor unions and trade organizations. They also worked with established labor unions to organize workers in the informal sector and advocated for policies and legislation to improve the rights, working conditions, and well-being of workers, including laborers in the informal sector. NGOs also collaborated with provincial governments to provide agricultural workers, brick kiln workers, and other vulnerable workers with national identification so workers could connect to the country's social safety net and access the benefits of citizenship (such as voting, health care, or education).

b. Prohibition of Forced or Compulsory Labor

The law prohibits all forms of forced or compulsory labor, cancels all existing bonded labor debts, forbids lawsuits for the recovery of such debts, and establishes a district "vigilance committee" system to implement the act. Federal and provincial acts, however, prohibit employees from leaving their employment without the consent of the employer, since doing so would subject them to penalties of imprisonment that could involve compulsory labor.

Lack of political will, the reported complicity of officials in trafficking, technical flaws in the law, federal and local government structural changes, and a lack of funds all contributed to the failure of authorities to enforce federal law relating to forced labor. Gaps also remained in the legislative framework. Consequently, when law enforcement officers registered bonded labor offenses, they did so under other sections of the penal code, including kidnapping and illegal confinement. Resources, inspections, and remediation were inadequate, and penalties--including a 50,000 rupee ($495) fine, two to five years' imprisonment, or both--were insufficient to deter violations.

The use of forced and bonded labor was widespread and common in many industries across the country. NGOs estimated nearly two million persons were in bondage, primarily in Sindh and Punjab, but also in Balochistan and KP. A large proportion of bonded laborers were low-caste Hindus, as well as Christians and Muslims with lower socioeconomic backgrounds. Bonded labor was common in the agricultural sector, including the cotton, sugarcane, and wheat industries, and in the brick, coal, glass, and carpet industries. Bonded laborers often were unable to determine when their debts were fully paid, in part because contracts were rare, and employers could take advantage of bonded laborers' illiteracy to alter debt amounts or the price laborers paid for seed and fertilizer. In some cases landowners restricted laborers' movements with armed guards or sold laborers to other employers for the price of the laborers' debts. The government of Punjab passed ordinances banning the employment of children in hazardous environments and a separate ordinance to prevent children from working in brick kilns. Enforcement was reportedly being carried out but not complete.

Boys and girls also were bought, sold, rented, or kidnapped to work in illegal begging rings, as domestic servants, or in agriculture, as bonded laborers (see section 7. c.). Illegal labor agents charged high fees to parents with false promises of decent work for their children and later exploited them by subjecting the children to forced labor in domestic servitude, unskilled labor, small shops, and other sectors.

Some bonded laborers returned to their former status after they were freed, due to a lack of alternative employment options. Ties between landowners, industry owners, and influential politicians hampered effective elimination of the problem.

For example, some local police did not pursue landowners or brick kiln owners effectively because they believed higher-ranking police, pressured by politicians or the owners themselves, would not support their efforts to carry out legal investigations.

The KP, Punjab, and Sindh ministries of labor were motivated to register brick kilns and their workers to regulate the industry better and provide workers access to labor courts and other services. Officials claimed they took steps to register brick kilns, but the exact number of registrations was not available. The Punjab Department of Labor ran a project to combat bonded labor in brick kilns by helping workers obtain national identity cards and interest-free loans; the department also opened schools at brick kiln sites and registered the children of brick kiln workers for school.

Also see the Department of State's *Trafficking in Persons Report* at www.state.gov/j/tip/rls/tiprpt/.

c. Prohibition of Child Labor and Minimum Age for Employment

The constitution expressly prohibits the employment of children below age 14 in any factory, mine, or other hazardous site. The national law for the employment of children set the minimum age for hazardous work at 15, an age not in compliance with international standards. The national law also does not establish a minimum age for employment in nonhazardous occupations. For children over 14, the law limits a child's workday to seven hours, including a one-hour break after three hours of labor, and sets permissible times of day for work and time off. The law does not allow children to work overtime or at night, and they should receive one day off per week. Additionally, the law requires employers to keep a register of child workers for labor inspectors to verify. These prohibitions and regulations, however, do not apply to family businesses or government schools.

The law prohibits the exploitation of children younger than age 18 and defines exploitative entertainment as all activities related to human sports or sexual practices and other abusive practices. Parents who exploit their children are legally liable. The law makes bonded labor of children punishable by up to five years in prison and 50,000 rupees ($495) in fines. The government prohibited the employment of children under age 15 in four occupations and 34 processes, including street vending, surgical instrument manufacturing, deep-sea fishing, leather manufacturing, brick making, soccer ball production, and carpet weaving. Despite these restrictions there were reports of children working in all these areas.

Coordination of child labor problems at the national level remained ineffective. As a result of devolution, labor inspection was carried out at the provincial rather than national level, which contributed to uneven application of labor law. Enforcement efforts were not adequate to meet the scale of the problem. Inspectors had little training and insufficient resources and were susceptible to corruption. Labor inspections became even less frequent after devolution, with no floor for the minimum frequency of inspections. Authorities allowed NGOs to perform inspections without interference, and SPARC noted that officials usually cooperated with its visits.

Authorities often did not impose penalties on violators; when they did, the penalties were not a significant deterrent. For example, while authorities obtained hundreds of convictions for violations of child labor laws, the fines were too low to deter future violations.

Due to weak government enforcement of child labor laws, child labor remained pervasive. According to the ILO, there were 3.4 million child laborers. In private briefings NGOs estimated the number to be significantly higher, with many children working in agriculture and domestic work.

Approximately 70 percent of nonagricultural child labor took place in small workshops, complicating efforts to enforce child labor laws, since by law inspectors may not inspect facilities employing fewer than 10 persons.

Employers and families forced children to work in brick kilns, and in the glass-bangle and carpet-weaving industries, as well as in agriculture, as part of fulfilling their families' debt obligation to landowners or brick kiln owners. UNICEF estimated the number of children working in brick kilns at 250,000. In 2012 researchers estimated there were approximately two million bonded laborers, many of whom included entire families with children. Children also reportedly worked in the production of incense, cotton, wheat textiles, tobacco, sugarcane, gemstones, and stone crushing.

Poor rural families sometimes sold their children into domestic servitude or other types of work, or they paid agents to arrange for such work, often believing their children would work under decent conditions. Some children sent to work for relatives or acquaintances in exchange for education or other opportunities ended in exploitative conditions or forced labor.

Children also were kidnapped or sold into organized begging rings, domestic servitude, militants and gangs, and child sex trafficking.

See the Department of Labor's *Findings on the Worst Forms of Child Labor* at www.dol.gov/ilab/reports/child-labor/findings/.

d. Discrimination with Respect to Employment and Occupation

While regulations prohibit discrimination in employment and occupation regarding race, sex, gender, disability, language, and gender identity, HIV-positive status or other communicable diseases, or social status, the government did not effectively enforce those laws and regulations.

Discrimination with respect to employment and occupation based on these factors persisted. The nature of penalties for violations was insufficient to deter violations.

e. Acceptable Conditions of Work

In July the government raised the minimum wage for unskilled workers from 13,000 ($125) rupees to 14,000 rupees ($135) per month, and all provincial governments budgets were required to follow that directive. While authorities increased the minimum wage in the annual budget, both federal and state governments also must issue required notifications for such increases to go into effect. Minimum wage laws did not cover significant sectors of the labor force-- including those in the informal sector, domestic servants, and agricultural workers.

The law provides for a maximum workweek of 48 hours (54 hours for seasonal factories) with rest periods during the workday and paid annual holidays. Additional benefits required under the labor code include official government holidays, overtime pay, annual and sick leave, health care, education for workers' children, social security, old age benefits, and a workers' welfare fund.

These regulations do not apply to agricultural workers, workers in factories with fewer than 10 employees, domestic workers, or contractors. These workers also lack the right to access "worker courts" to seek redress of grievances and were otherwise extremely vulnerable to exploitation. The inapplicability of many labor laws and the lack of enforcement by the government gave employers in many sectors relative impunity with regard to working conditions, treatment of employees, work hours, and pay.

Provincial governments have primary responsibility for enforcing national labor regulations. Enforcement was ineffective due to limited resources, corruption, and inadequate regulatory structures. In Sindh Province policies against surprise inspections severely limited effective enforcement. In Punjab a system whereby owners voluntarily posted their own declarations about workplace safety, health, and wage issues in their factories replaced routine inspections. Officials then chose factories at random for inspection. Balochistan and KP allowed surprise inspections. Many workers, especially in the informal sectors, remained unaware of their rights. In face of the serious restrictions on labor inspections and the effect of limited resources and corruption, inspections and penalties were insufficient to deter violations of labor laws.

Health and safety standards were poor in all sectors. There was a serious lack of adherence to mine-safety and health protocols. Many mines had only one opening for entry, egress, and ventilation. Workers could not remove themselves from dangerous working conditions without risking loss of employment. Informal sector employees faced multiple precarious situations, particularly in less visible areas such as domestic work. There were no official statistics on workplace fatalities and accidents during the year.

The country's failure to meet international health and safety standards raised doubts abroad as to its reliability as a source for imports. The Sindh government consulted with the ILO to develop a program to improve its labor standards and laws in an attempt to regain its status as an export source. Following the 2012 fire at a Karachi textile factory that killed 259 persons, some labor advocates complained that many families had not received their promised compensation and that the factors that led to the tragedy--most notably a fraudulent safety certification and inadequate fire safety measures--existed at many other companies.

www.ingramcontent.com/pod-product-compliance
Lightning Source LLC
Chambersburg PA
CBHW070815280726
48660CB00015B/859